2ND EDITION

Small-Group Reading Instruction

A Differentiated Teaching Model for Beginning and Struggling Readers

Beverly Tyner

International Reading Association
800 BARKSDALE ROAD, PO BOX 8139
NEWARK, DE 19714-8139, USA
www.reading.org

The International Reading Association attempts, through its publications, to provide a forum for a wide spectrum of opinions on reading. This policy permits divergent viewpoints without implying the endorsement of the Association.

Executive Editor, Books   Corinne M. Mooney
Developmental Editor   Charlene M. Nichols
Developmental Editor   Tori Mello Bachman
Developmental Editor   Stacey L. Reid
Editorial Production Manager   Shannon T. Fortner
Design and Composition Manager   Anette Schuetz

Project Editors   Charlene M. Nichols and Rebecca A. Fetterolf

Cover   Design, Monotype; Photographs, Katrina Gravitte

The publisher would appreciate notification where errors occur so that they may be corrected in subsequent printings and/or editions.

Library of Congress Cataloging-in-Publication Data

Tyner, Beverly.
 Small-group reading instruction : a differentiated teaching model for beginning and struggling readers / Beverly Tyner. -- 2nd ed.
     p. cm.
 Includes bibliographical references and index.
 ISBN 978-0-87207-709-6
 1. Reading (Elementary) 2. Group reading. 3. Reading--Remedial teaching. I. Title.
 LB1573.T96 2009
 372.41'62--dc22
                                                                            2009003145

To my mother, Helen Davis Bernard, who remains a champion for the "struggling reader" and most of all a champion for her family

CONTENTS

Beverly Tyner, EdD, is an educator with more than 30 years of experience. Her career includes positions as a teacher, principal, and school district curriculum director. She was also a graduate professor and the director of student teaching at Kennesaw State University in Atlanta, Georgia, USA.

In 2004, Beverly published her first book, *Small-Group Reading Instruction: A Differentiated Teaching Model for Beginning and Struggling Readers,* with the International Reading Association. In 2005, she published a sequel to her first book: *Small-Group Reading Instruction: A Differentiated Teaching Model for Intermediate Readers, Grades 3–8.* Beverly has also produced training DVDs that accompany her books. In addition, Beverly has published research in the *Journal of Educational Psychology* that supports her reading intervention model.

Currently, Beverly is a private literacy consultant. Her work includes presenting at national and international conferences, consulting with schools and school districts, and writing curriculum materials. Beverly is also a staff developer and presenter with the Bureau of Education Research. Most recently, she has been assisting school districts with the implementation of Response to Intervention (RTI) using her reading intervention model. Beverly is well known for her practical yet research-based models in reading instruction. She feels that her most important work continues to be with students and teachers within the classroom setting.

Beverly resides in Chattanooga, Tennessee, with her husband, Paul, and is the mother of four children, including three college students and a missionary.

Author Information for Correspondence and Workshops

Beverly presents at national and international conferences, consults with schools and school districts, and writes curriculum materials. Beverly is also a staff developer and presenter. She can be reached at www.literacylinks.net.

FOREWORD

Small-Group Reading Instruction, by Dr. Beverly Tyner, needs no introduction to the reading education community. Originally published in 2004, the book quickly became a nationwide "best seller" in the International Reading Association's publication series. Unlike many teaching guides, Dr. Tyner's book did not emerge from—or attempt to capitalize on—one of the frequently changing trends in the field of beginning reading (i.e., "What's hot, what's not?"). Instead, the book emerged from a sound theory of early reading development and grassroots, trial-and-error testing of that theory in real classrooms. It is this theory-into-practice quality that defines Dr. Tyner's contribution.

In the late 1990s, Dr. Tyner participated in Early Steps, a research-tested, early intervention program for at-risk first-grade readers (Morris, Tyner, & Perney, 2000; Santa & Høien, 1999). For two years, she taught struggling readers, herself, and trained other teachers to use the Early Steps intervention. Then she went further. Dr. Tyner adapted the Early Steps teaching components (e.g., rereadings, sentence writing, word study, introducing a new story) so that they could be used successfully in a small-group context. This was an important achievement. Her resulting book, Small-Group Reading Instruction, featured effective assessments and a balanced instructional scheme (guided reading, phonics, and writing). Moreover, the book met an important need in the first decade of the 2000s, providing teachers with a practical blueprint for differentiating reading instruction in the classroom.

Over the past 5 years, Dr. Tyner has traveled throughout the United States helping teachers to apply the ideas in her teaching model. This second edition of her book clearly demonstrates her involvement with practicing teachers. Certain assessments and teaching techniques have been revised, and there is a new chapter on classroom management; that is, how to engage other students in meaningful, independent activities when the teacher is working with a small reading group.

In the new era of Response to Intervention (RTI), classroom and reading teachers are being asked to use instructional interventions to (1) accelerate the progress of struggling readers and (2) ascertain the severity of specific children's reading problems. To accomplish these goals, teachers will need more than "scientifically-based" boxes and kits of materials; they will need knowledge (theoretical and practical). In the best of worlds, such pedagogical knowledge is developed through careful clinical training, such as that which led Dr. Tyner to write her book. In the absence of such training, primary-grade teachers can turn to Small-Group Reading Instruction, a helpful book rooted in sound theory and practice, and written by a dedicated educator.

Darrell Morris
Appalachian State University
Boone, North Carolina, USA

PREFACE

Since the publication of *Small-Group Reading Instruction: A Differentiated Teaching Model for Beginning and Struggling Readers* in 2004, I have had the opportunity to work with thousands of teachers and students in a continual quest to adjust the Small-Group Differentiated Teaching Model in terms of student engagement and to incorporate current reading research. My original purpose in writing *Small-Group Reading Instruction* was to present a powerful model for teachers who worked with beginning readers in kindergarten through second grade or struggling readers through fifth grade. That purpose has not changed. In my nearly 35 years as a teacher, principal, reading specialist, university professor, and national literacy consultant, I have had the privilege of working in more than 30 states and in several countries. My primary observation in these varied experiences is the desperate needs of both students and teachers in the area of beginning reading instruction. Most recently, I've observed that many districts are purchasing and in some cases are being forced to purchase boxed reading programs with promises of the delivery of research-based instruction. Boxed reading programs that do not provide teachers with the appropriate materials or the necessary knowledge about the development of readers will never be the answer for struggling readers. In addition, teachers and students continue to be saddled with basal reading programs with promises of adhering to the program and "everyone will be successful." Although basal programs have components that are useful, again they must be tempered with knowledge of the individual readers and the appropriate teaching venues through which these readers should be taught. Empowering teachers with the knowledge to be good consumers of reading products and materials will, in my opinion, drive the reading process forward in an unprecedented way.

Effective reading instruction comprises guided contextual reading and systematic word study that is skillfully paced to the rate of individual students. This type of teaching and learning is most effective when instruction is delivered in the smallest grouping possible so as to best address students' specific literacy needs. Providing such instruction in the primary classroom, which often ranges from 24 to 28 students, is increasingly difficult. Many basal readers provide a limited number of leveled readers, and the books are often insufficient in addressing the wide range of readers in most classrooms. In addition, many teachers feel that they lack the training and are not fully prepared to teach reading to a wide range of readers in their classrooms who are left struggling in programs that rely solely on basal readers. Those students who read significantly above or below grade level fail to thrive. With the expectation that all students progress regardless of their reading levels, small-group instruction is the only practical way to realistically meet the needs of diverse readers.

Tutorial programs such Reading Recovery (Clay, 1993) and Early Steps (Morris, Tyner, & Perney, 2000) have been successful with individual students in schools where sufficient funds have been available. Students in these programs are typically taken out of the regular classroom and given 30 minutes of one-on-one reading instruction on a daily basis.

However, a comparable model for small-group instruction in the regular classroom setting has been lacking. There is no question that one-on-one quality tutoring provides the most effective delivery system for struggling readers (Morris et al., 2000; Santa, 1999), but the cost for such programs makes them impractical. Federal mandates such as Response to Intervention point to the urgency of a research-based small-group instructional model that can be implemented in the regular classroom setting and in additional reading interventions for struggling readers.

For the past 16 years, I have focused my attention on the development of a small-group comprehensive reading model that would provide effective reading instruction for all students. Although I have a great deal of respect for the complexities of reading and writing and the research that surrounds it, my primary concern in writing and revising this book is to meld the research into a model that brings simplicity and usability. As I continue to review the research that surrounds this important topic, I remain confident that the Small-Group Differentiated Reading Model is intrinsically steeped in the most current reading research–based practices. Perhaps more important, I know that these strategies work, as evidenced in research (Morris et al., 2000; National Institute of Child Health and Human Development, 2000; Santa, 1999) as well as in the daily successes of the students I have observed participating in this model.

Although the foundation of this reading model has for the most part stayed the same, this second edition contains some important changes. Additions include a complete scope and sequence for word study that supports systematic and explicit instruction. Also included are simple word study assessments that can assist teachers in making informed decisions in planning for powerful instruction, as well as assessments that offer the ability to monitor progress in critical literacy areas that support more focused instruction. In response to teacher requests, additional independent literacy activities that support the reading research–based strategies are included for each developmental stage. These activities are simple, yet powerful and easy to manage. You will also find numerous modifications and suggestions throughout that will hopefully lead to more engagement for both teachers and students.

Small-Group Reading Instruction can be used for a variety of purposes. Although intended primarily for use by classroom teachers in kindergarten through second grade and by reading specialists and special education teachers, it also provides a solid basis for reading instruction in teacher preparation programs. It can also be used as a book study for professional learning communities. Finally, this book can be used in reading intervention programs with individuals or small groups of beginning or struggling readers, including English-language learner and special education populations throughout the elementary grades.

My greatest pleasure over the past five years has been to observe the successes of both teachers and students who have embraced the Small-Group Differentiated Reading Model. My focus has been to continually seek the most effective research-based strategies to support teachers and increase student achievement. With an ever-shrinking instructional day, it has become imperative—now more than ever before—to examine each and every strategy and activity for effectiveness. Our two most valuable recourses in the teaching of reading are the time we spend in direct instruction and the quality of our instructional delivery. I sincerely hope that the revisions I have made to this book will assist teachers in their goal of becoming powerful reading teachers for all students.

ACKNOWLEDGMENTS

During the 1997–1999 school years, it was my great pleasure to work alongside Darrell Morris, professor of reading at Appalachian State University, as he trained reading tutors in my school district. His work is the guiding force behind my efforts in writing this book. Along with his extensive knowledge of the reading process, Darrell brings a personal dedication to providing effective reading instruction to all beginning readers. Darrell and I conducted a research study that documented the success of his reading intervention model, Early Steps, in a large, urban district (Morris et al., 2000). Much of the information in this book is based on the work of Darrell, whose sincere desire to share with others brings a rare authenticity to his craft.

I cannot overlook the hundreds of teachers who have worked with me over the past years in perfecting this model. Their excitement and dedication to the teaching of reading inspires me on a daily basis and motivated me to publish this book. It is, I am convinced, in the "everydayness" of the classroom that real research takes place.

I also would like to thank my four precious children—Leslie, Susan, Jennifer, and Harrison—who taught me a great deal about the reading process. In addition, I would like to thank my husband, Paul, who was once a struggling reader, and his mother, Polly, who was relentless in finding him the help he needed. Paul's remarkable successes both personally and professionally are an inspiration to others who struggle in reading. Thank you for your unwavering support of my work. More important, thank you for being an incredible father and husband. There is no one else I would rather pull the midnight shift with.

CHAPTER 1

Beginning Reading Instruction and the Small-Group Differentiated Reading Model

Over the past 15 years, there has been an unprecedented focus on the teaching of beginning reading. Although much has been accomplished, most educators would agree that we are continuing to fail too many struggling readers. Teachers are passionate about early reading success because they know that it is the cornerstone upon which knowledge, self-esteem, and future educational opportunities are built. Our students' futures are all but determined by how well they learn to read. In the United States, which offers few career opportunities for the illiterate, teaching children to read proficiently is the most important single task in education. The consequences of these literacy deficits are devastating to those students who are ill prepared for further educational opportunities and ultimately the world of work. Research is clear about the need for early, effective reading instruction. The National Institute of Child Health and Human Development (NICHD; 2000) finds that low-performing first-grade readers will likely be the lowest performing readers into adulthood. If teachers are to make achieving high literacy levels a reality for all children, the instruction must begin when students enter the school door. As students matriculate through the grades, an ever-growing chasm between proficient and nonproficient readers widens. Although teachers know a great deal about the reading process, many questions remain concerning the most effective methods to use when instructing children. I have encountered many teachers who remain frustrated by the lack of quality materials available for beginning reading instruction or who are led astray by boxed reading programs that typically don't meet their promises. Moreover, teachers often commented that they were poorly prepared in their undergraduate training to meet the needs of beginning and struggling readers in their classrooms. The Small-Group Differentiated Reading Model presented in this book supports teachers by presenting easy-to-implement lesson plans that incorporate reading research–based strategies for teaching beginning reading. This model will give each student the opportunity to grow as a reader.

Children begin their formal literacy journey when they enter school, whether in a preschool or kindergarten program. Beginning this journey requires teachers to assess each student's literacy knowledge and provide the appropriate instruction that will advance the child's literacy learning. Students enter a typical kindergarten class with very different levels of printed-language knowledge, and instruction must be adapted for these differences. Implementing the components of a balanced literacy model, including small-group differentiated reading, is an effective way to provide appropriate instruction. Some educators feel that small-group reading instruction is inappropriate for young children.

On the contrary, young children deserve the same literacy opportunities as older children. For example, those students entering school with alphabet and sound knowledge should progress to the next step in the reading process. The "letter of the week" curriculum is no longer adequate in launching students into a literate world. Numerous young children are often left behind when they fail to acquire skills and knowledge critical to literacy development such as the ability to track print, alphabet knowledge, and phonemic awareness. Traditionally, instruction in these areas has taken place in a whole-class setting with little regard for individual student needs. Students who matriculate to first grade without solid literacy foundations often struggle to catch up.

Beyond the Basal for Beginning Readers

Basal reading programs remain the dominant means of reading instruction in the United States. A basal reading series was never intended to provide a complete program, only the framework. Many textbook companies tout their ability to provide all the tools necessary for providing effective reading instruction for a wide range of readers in whole-group, small-group, and intervention settings. In my opinion, this has not been the case. Basal readers are most effective when they are used flexibly and as part of a comprehensive, balanced program of instruction. Conversely, basal readers are least effective when they are used as the total reading program. This is true for all levels of readers but has particular implications for beginning and struggling readers.

The most overlooked component in current basal series is an effective small-group reading model with appropriately leveled texts accompanied by a developmental word study focus. Although some basal programs give lip service to small-group instruction, the materials and guidance necessary for successful implementation are often lacking. Recently, textbook companies have boarded the "leveled reading bandwagon" in an attempt to fill this void. Generally, these resources include one additional book below grade level, one book on grade level, and one book above grade level. In most classrooms, these materials are not sufficient in addressing an ever-growing diverse reading population. In most instances, the accompanying lesson plans are brief and generally focus on whole-group comprehension and word study strategies. These models lack the intensity, focus, and developmental sequence necessary to clearly address the needs of beginning and struggling readers.

It is not advantageous for textbook companies to support an extensive small-group reading model that requires school districts to purchase numerous books because it would be cost prohibitive. Additionally, basal word study is presented in a grade-level scope and sequence that ignores those students who have gaps in their word study knowledge or have already mastered the grade-level standards. Textbook companies are in a competitive market, and, therefore, they try to present the most economical program. As consumers, we must remember that without carefully leveled reading materials and developmental word study to supplement the basal, it is impossible to adequately meet the needs of a wide range of readers.

Children in the early stages of literacy development have unique needs. If children are to seek hungrily for literacy, they must experience early success in beginning reading.

Typically, the basal reader covers one story a week. Limiting a child to reading one story a week—a text that may or may not be at the appropriate instructional level—limits the child's ability to reach higher levels of achievement. The instructional level of reading is the highest level at which a student can read with support from the teacher, usually a text read with somewhere between 93% and 97% accuracy. Reading and rereading a variety of texts at appropriate levels drives instruction forward for all students.

Perhaps the group most neglected in a basal-only reading program is struggling readers. High achievers are capable of reading the weekly story before it is introduced; therefore, these students flourish in spite of the system. Average students probably fare best within the basal reading model, although they too are limited by reading opportunities. Struggling readers, on the other hand, are the clear losers in a basal-only classroom. More often than not, their only reading instruction is presented at a level of frustration—the level at which they cannot comfortably succeed. This then begins the downward spiral; motivation is lost and the gap between readers and nonreaders widens.

Gaps in Other Small-Group Reading Models

Significant attention has been given to small-group reading during the last 12 years. The developers of guided reading, Fountas and Pinnell (1996), should be applauded for their contributions to this important small-group reading process. It was, in fact, the only reading model that attempted to instruct children in a small group at an appropriate instructional reading level for numerous years. The goal of this "guided" reading model is "to help children learn how to use independent reading strategies successfully" (p. 2), which focuses primarily on comprehension strategies. It could, therefore, be interpreted that this type of guided reading is most appropriate for those students who already have mastered basic decoding skills such as concepts of print, letter sounds, sight words, or basic phonics and have reached somewhat independent reading levels. Although the ultimate goal of any reading program is to comprehend text, basic foundational decoding skills cannot be overlooked. What happens to those readers who lack the prerequisite skills that are needed for reading? Providing reading instruction that takes a student from a nonreader to reader status is a skilled process. Many beginning readers require focused instruction that includes alphabet knowledge, phonemic awareness, phonics, or even the ability to track simple lines of print. It is our responsibility as teachers to determine the developmental needs of each student in the beginning reading process and offer instruction necessary to advance his or her literacy learning.

Although "guided reading" and other basal-driven small-group models present some excellent strategies, there are some deficits in these models that cannot be ignored. The accompanying systematic word study, vocabulary, and oral reading fluency strategies are necessary to complete the literacy framework. Most basal-driven small-group models use limited leveled books and do not differentiate for word study levels. In addition, these small-group models lack the frequency and explicit teaching that beginning readers require. Table 1 shows the similarities and differences among guided reading; basal, small-group reading; and the Small-Group Differentiated Reading Model presented in this book. Although it might be argued that word study and writing are taught during another part of the school

Comparing Traditional Guided Reading; Basal, Small-Group Reading; and the Small-Group Differentiated Reading Model

Traditional Guided Reading	Basal, Small-Group Reading	Small-Group Differentiated Reading Model
Students grouped according to reading level	Grouped three ways: below, at, or above grade level	Students grouped according to reading and word study level
Uses leveled books	Offers one leveled book per week per group	Uses numerous leveled books
Comprehension focus	Reinforces whole-group comprehension and word study focus	Decoding and comprehension focuses
No systematic word study component		Variety of reading strategies used (whisper, partner, and choral reading)
No writing component		Systematic word study (beginning with alphabet knowledge and continuing through variant vowel patterns)
No word bank		Writing (beginning with shared writing and progressing to independent writing)
		Vocabulary (automatic recognition of basic sight words and words in text)

day, the effectiveness of this instruction in the context of whole-class instruction with little regard for individual needs is questionable. Until a child becomes an independent reader, word study and writing are so closely linked in the developmental reading process that they are most effectively taught in a systematic way that supports each child's reading level and builds a solid decoding as well as comprehension foundation. Although the traditional guided reading model as well as basal, small-group models have much to offer, we cannot ignore potential instructional gaps for beginning readers. As a parent, teacher, administrator, and reading specialist, I have observed that a more explicit small-group reading model is necessary, especially as it applies to beginning and struggling readers.

The Small-Group Differentiated Reading Model

Development of the Model

My interest in developing a specific small-group differentiated reading model resulted from my work as a reading specialist in a large, urban school district in the southeastern

United States. Along with other urban districts, our district was experiencing an ever-increasing number of students reading below grade level. In an attempt to reduce these reading failures, a search began for an early, intensive reading intervention model that could assist numerous students. The Reading Recovery model (Clay, 1993) was quickly ruled out because of the program's high cost and inability to serve more than a few students dictated by the program guidelines. However, Early Steps, a reading intervention model developed by Darrell Morris, met the criteria. Reading tutors, assistants, and volunteers could be trained in this early intervention model, and numerous at-risk students could be served.

Early Steps, a one-on-one tutoring intervention, is based on research and best practices in reading instruction, including rereading, word study, and writing as integral parts. Most important, reading tutors are trained on site in an apprenticeship format. First-grade students in our district made impressive gains as a result of the implementation of Early Steps (see Morris et al., 2000). Although the intervention was successful for individual students, the basal reading program continued to be ineffective in meeting the needs of students in the classroom. Whole-class instruction and a lack of appropriately leveled books left teachers frustrated.

Using the components of Early Steps, I set out to develop a small-group differentiated instructional model that would address the needs of beginning and struggling readers in the regular classroom setting or in reading intervention. The Small-Group Differentiated Reading Model (see Figure 1) provides a systematic framework for teaching beginning and struggling readers. It takes into consideration the developmental stages through which readers progress, the critical research-based components for reading success, and the time needed to develop these literacy foundations.

What Is Differentiated Reading Instruction?

As many schools continue to move toward adapting to an ever-increasing broad range of learners, it becomes more important than ever to develop instruction to respond to these academically diverse students. Differentiating instruction for beginning readers is one step to appropriately address the academic diversity that exists in virtually every primary classroom. Quite simply, differentiation means modifying instruction based on student readiness. A research study in Texas revealed that there was typically a four-year grade span between the lowest and highest readers in first-grade classrooms (Guszak, as cited in Texas Reading Initiative: Differentiated Instruction). Differentiating reading instruction enables teachers to plan strategically so that they can meet the needs of both weaker and stronger students.

At its core, the model of differentiated reading presented in this book uses research-based components and strategies in beginning reading instruction and developmental models that recognize the stages through which beginning readers naturally progress. Readers and nonreaders have been typically categorized as either one group or the other with little regard for the in-between group in which many beginning and struggling readers are often trapped. Reading is not an all-or-nothing skill: Alphabet knowledge, phonemic awareness, phonics, print-related knowledge, word recognition, fluency, and

FIGURE 1
The Small-Group Differentiated Reading Model

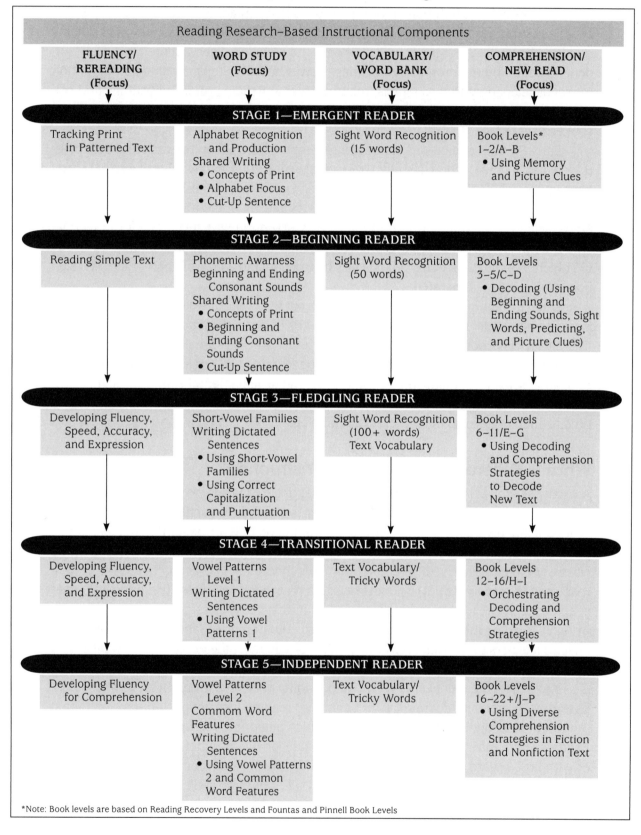

Reading Research–Based Instructional Components			
FLUENCY/ REREADING (Focus)	**WORD STUDY** (Focus)	**VOCABULARY/ WORD BANK** (Focus)	**COMPREHENSION/ NEW READ** (Focus)
STAGE 1—EMERGENT READER			
Tracking Print in Patterned Text	Alphabet Recognition and Production Shared Writing • Concepts of Print • Alphabet Focus • Cut-Up Sentence	Sight Word Recognition (15 words)	Book Levels* 1–2/A–B • Using Memory and Picture Clues
STAGE 2—BEGINNING READER			
Reading Simple Text	Phonemic Awarness Beginning and Ending Consonant Sounds Shared Writing • Concepts of Print • Beginning and Ending Consonant Sounds • Cut-Up Sentence	Sight Word Recognition (50 words)	Book Levels 3–5/C–D • Decoding (Using Beginning and Ending Sounds, Sight Words, Predicting, and Picture Clues)
STAGE 3—FLEDGLING READER			
Developing Fluency, Speed, Accuracy, and Expression	Short-Vowel Families Writing Dictated Sentences • Using Short-Vowel Families • Using Correct Capitalization and Punctuation	Sight Word Recognition (100+ words) Text Vocabulary	Book Levels 6–11/E–G • Using Decoding and Comprehension Strategies to Decode New Text
STAGE 4—TRANSITIONAL READER			
Developing Fluency, Speed, Accuracy, and Expression	Vowel Patterns Level 1 Writing Dictated Sentences • Using Vowel Patterns 1	Text Vocabulary/ Tricky Words	Book Levels 12–16/H–I • Orchestrating Decoding and Comprehension Strategies
STAGE 5—INDEPENDENT READER			
Developing Fluency for Comprehension	Vowel Patterns Level 2 Commom Word Features Writing Dictated Sentences • Using Vowel Patterns 2 and Common Word Features	Text Vocabulary/ Tricky Words	Book Levels 16–22+/J–P • Using Diverse Comprehension Strategies in Fiction and Nonfiction Text

*Note: Book levels are based on Reading Recovery Levels and Fountas and Pinnell Book Levels comprehension are all integral parts. This is the basis for the Small-Group Differentiated Reading Model. The question then becomes, Where along the reading continuum does each reader fall? Whenever a teacher reaches out to a small reading group to vary teaching techniques and strategies to create the best teaching experience possible, differentiated instruction takes place.

Children enter the classroom with a variety of background experiences. For children with numerous prior experiences with print, many of the early reading processes may already be mastered. In contrast, children who enter with relatively no knowledge about print will require a different instructional plan. Without differentiated reading instruction, some children will fall further behind whereas others will be left unchallenged. In reading instruction, the gap between poor and good readers widens with each subsequent year (National Center for Education Statistics, 2001). The Small-Group Differentiated Reading Model includes a variety of reading strategies based on the developmental needs of the reader, not on the chronological age or grade level. Although accommodating student differences might be difficult at times, they must be recognized and addressed. If we are sincere about having students achieve higher standards and having the best interest of each student at heart, we must differentiate instructional reading strategies. Students start at different points in the reading process, and we must provide the most appropriate level of challenge to increase their literacy learning.

The Small-Group Differentiated Reading Model presented in Figure 1 is differentiated in two important ways. First, the five stages in the beginning reading process—emergent reader, beginning reader, fledgling reader, transitional reader, and independent reader—are clearly differentiated as a reader progresses toward independence. Additionally, the instructional components—fluency, word study, vocabulary, and comprehension—are addressed for each stage of development, which included both encoding and decoding strategies. Although there remains some contention concerning these two predominant methods of reading instruction, it is time to recognize the common ground that research clearly supports: a need for both strategies to be taught.

Differentiating the Stages of Beginning Reading

Reading is a complex process with many steps and variables. However, the road to reading has some definite milestones through which readers must navigate. Beginning readers are often lumped together with little delineation of differences, yet these differences are critical to the reading process and should not be ignored. For example, students who are struggling in the classroom are often grouped together for reading intervention. These struggling readers should be assessed and placed with students who are most similar in their literacy needs in order to make adequate gains in reading.

In most primary classrooms, some students struggle with reading, others perform well beyond grade-level expectations, and the rest fall somewhere in between. By differentiating the stages of reading instruction through flexible small groups, the diverse needs of a heterogeneous group can best be met. This differentiated reading model recognizes the developmental stages through which a reader progresses and adapts instructional strategies to support the reader in each stage. Allowing for flexible small-group reading instruction in primary classrooms where some students struggle and others perform well beyond grade-level expectations provides appropriate instruction for all readers.

To effectively guide the reading process, first there must be an understanding of the stages in beginning reading and the print demands placed on a reader at these different stages. For example, in the early stages of reading, there is a heavier emphasis on decoding than on comprehension. Contextual reading, writing, spelling, sight word recognition, and phonics develop simultaneously in predictable stages. Table 2 details the five stages that are addressed in the Small-Group Differentiated Reading Model. Appropriate grade-level designations are given for each of the reading stages along with the beginning student characteristics and major focuses of each stage. This progression begins in Stage 1 with the emergent reader (basically nonreader) and continues to an independent reading level in Stage 5. Students advance through these levels as they build on their knowledge and move forward at their own pace. These five stages serve as the framework for the Small-Group Differentiated Reading Model presented in this book and will be discussed thoroughly in Chapters 4 through 8.

Reading Research–Based Components of Effective Reading Instruction

Many educators and parents have been and continue to be frustrated with or confused about the wide swings in the reading instruction pendulum. A team of U.S. national education associations observed,

> The famous pendulum of educational innovation swings more widely on reading than in any other subject. Pendulum swings of this kind are characteristic of fields driven by fashion, not evidence. Hemlines go up and down because of changing tastes, not new evidence; progress in medicine, engineering, and agriculture, based to a far degree on evidence from rigorous research, is both faster and less subject to radical shifts. In the same way, educational practice must come to be based on evidence—not ideology. (Learning First Alliance, 1998, p. 18)

Typically, when a particular strategy or approach in reading fails to teach some children how to read, educators respond by changing instructional approaches. Unfortunately, the new approach may prove to be effective with only a portion of students, and educators scurry back to the first approach. This is particularly evident as it relates to special needs students and English-language learners (ELLs). Many times educators search for "magic bullets" to fix students and abandon best practices in reading instruction. In most instances, these struggling readers simply need more time spent in explicit research-based reading instruction.

Few educators would argue that good reading instruction includes a combination of strategies to teach all children to read. A differentiated approach that includes the best research practices will more likely meet a much wider range of learners (NICHD, 2000). The Small-Group Differentiated Reading Model attempts to capture the best practices in reading instruction for beginning readers through the integration of carefully differentiated

TABLE 2
Stages of Beginning Reading

Stage	Appropriate Grade Level	Beginning Student Characteristics	Major Focuses
1 Emergent Reader	Pre-K/Early K	• Knows less than half of the alphabet • Has no concept of word • Has little phonemic awareness • Recognizes few or no sight words	• Using memory and pictures • Recognizing and reproducing letters of the alphabet • Tracking print • Recognizing 15 sight words
2 Beginning Reader	Mid K/Late K	• Knows half or more of the alphabet • Has the ability to track print • Is able to hear some sounds • Recognizes 15 sight words	• Completing alphabet recognition and production • Using beginning and ending consonant sounds • Recognizing 50 sight words • Reading simple text • Using sentence context and pictures or word recognition cues to decode
3 Fledgling Reader	Early/Mid First Grade	• Confirms with beginning and ending consonant sounds • Recognizes 50+ sight words • Reads simple text	• Recognizing and using word families in reading and writing • Recognizing 100+ sight words • Reading more complex text • Developing fluency • Developing comprehension strategies • Self-correcting errors
4 Transitional Reader	Mid/Late First Grade	• Recognizes word families in isolation and in texts • Recognizes 100+ sight words • Reads developed text	• Using common vowel patterns in reading and writing • Developing independent reading using decoding and comprehension strategies • Developing fluency
5 Independent Reader	Early/Late Second Grade	• Reads and writes independently • Uses strategies to figure out new words • Reads fluently • Uses common vowel patterns and word features in reading and writing	• Developing diverse comprehension strategies • Using complex vowel patterns • Developing fluency in a variety of texts • Responding to text in a variety of ways

instructional strategies in each lesson. Rather than relying on one approach or another, each strategy has been carefully weighed in relation to research and its importance to the reading process. Although Chapter 2 will address the specific instructional strategies and activities as they relate to the models and stages of reading development, it is important to discuss the most recent research-based components and their importance to a comprehensive reading model.

Most reading researchers as well as practitioners acknowledge that the teaching of reading is multifaceted; there are no quick or easy fixes. There is, however, a recognized set of instructional components that are imperative to the teaching of reading. The most current and comprehensive examination of these reading components was completed by the National Reading Panel and released in the year 2000 (NICHD, 2000). The panel reviewed the reading research for the foundational years of kindergarten through eighth grade to identify components that consistently relate to reading success. These five components were identified as (1) phonemic awareness, (2) phonics, (3) fluency, (4) vocabulary, and (5) comprehension. To understand the importance of this research, a brief discussion of each component will be presented with implications for whole-group and small-group differentiated reading instruction.

Phonemic Awareness

Phonemic awareness is the understanding that the sounds of spoken language work together to make words. Most important, to benefit from phonics instruction a student needs to demonstrate phonemic awareness. Students who exhibit phonemic awareness will have an easier time learning to read and spell (Goswami, 2002). Phonemic awareness is a subset of a larger category called phonological awareness that includes identifying rhymes and syllables and manipulating sounds and is not included in the research base. Therefore, this discussion only relates to the strategies needed for students to accrue phonemic awareness. According to research, phonemic awareness can be taught and learned (Armbruster, Lehr, & Osborn, 2001).

Implications for Whole-Group Reading Instruction

Phonemic awareness is a grade-level benchmark for both kindergarten and first-grade students. Therefore, the strategies needed to acquire these skills should be taught explicitly in whole-group instruction. Songs, rhymes, and stories provide rich content for teaching phonemic awareness in whole-group instruction. Additionally, phonemic awareness is practiced by segmenting and blending words as these early readers begin to read and spell.

Implications for Small-Group Differentiated Reading Instruction

Research is clear that small-group instruction is effective in helping students to acquire phonemic awareness (Morris et al., 2000; NICHD, 2000; Santa & Høien, 1999). Although some students acquire this important skill set through whole-group exposure, many students still lack this important foundational knowledge. Therefore, small-group differentiated reading instruction provides phonemic awareness in an explicit and systematic format.

Blending and segmenting sounds in words as well as isolating initial sounds are strategies used in the small-group model. The beginning and fledging reader stages include strategies that support the development of phonemic awareness.

Phonics and Word Study

The term *phonics* falls under the wider category called *word study*. Word study refers to the systematic, developmental study of words. Word study for beginning and struggling readers encompasses alphabet knowledge, beginning consonant sounds, word families, common and uncommon vowel patterns, as well as simple word features such as prefixes and suffixes. For the purposes of this text, the term *word study* will be inclusive of these components. The purpose of phonics instruction is not to teach students to sound out words but to give students strategies so they learn to recognize words quickly and automatically, thereby increasing their reading fluency and comprehension.

Although the strategies and routines for the word study component will be reviewed in Chapters 4 through 8, it is important to examine the significance of word study in the reading process. According to Bear, Invernizzi, and Johnston (2004), the most critical factor behind fluent word reading is the ability to recognize letters, spelling patterns, and whole words effortlessly. Further, Bear and colleagues state that the ability to use phonics seems to depend on whether or how a child has been taught phonics. The National Reading Panel report (NICHD, 2000) points out that when phonics and word study are taught explicitly and systematically, not only kindergartners but even preschoolers, special needs students, and students through the eighth grade can successfully use this method to learn new words. Explicit, systematic phonics is a powerful mode of teaching young or slow learners. Additionally, students who have completed a basic phonics program benefit from the more advanced study of word features.

Implications for Whole-Group Reading Instruction

Basic phonics instruction is generally completed in two years for average students (generally mid-kindergarten through mid–second grade). After this foundational phonics knowledge is mastered, the study of word features continues through upper elementary and middle school. Grade-level standards dictate that much of this be taught in whole-group instruction. A phonics component can be found in most published reading basal series but, in my opinion, lack a logical scope and sequence and intensity and, therefore, fail to meet the developmental needs of all students. Whether teaching a systematic basal sequence or an alternative, this whole-group phonics instruction should address grade-level standards and be planned with systematic delivery. Additionally, a systematic word study component should continue as they relate to grade-level standards through middle school.

Implications for Small-Group Differentiated Reading Instruction

The need for systematic phonics and word study instruction delivered in a small-group setting is well documented (Morris et al., 2000; NICHD, 2000; Santa & Høien, 1999). In my opinion, it is the missing ingredient in most small-group models. Differentiated instruction demands that this crucial component be delivered with the same level of concern and attention as an appropriate reading level. After administering word study assessments (see Chapter 3), teachers determine appropriate word study levels to accommodate readers in small-group instruction. This provides readers who missed important phonics or word study components taught in whole-group instruction opportunities for additional time to master these basic skills. Furthermore, students who have progressed further in the word study sequence will be able to move at an accelerated rate in the study of prefixes, suffixes, complex patterns, and Greek and Latin roots.

Fluency (Rereading)

Research is clear about the need to develop fluency in readers through rereading (Chard, Vaughn, & Tyler, 2002). Fluency is the vehicle that takes the child from focusing on the words to focusing on the meaning of the text. Quite simply, practicing reading makes better, more confident readers. As students reread, they are able to increase their speed, use phrasing techniques, and become more automatic with the reading process. Automaticity is essential to reading success. Automaticity refers to how quickly or automatically students can recognize words so they can focus on the meaning of the text.

Repeated reading is an excellent technique for helping children achieve automaticity in reading. Repeated reading facilitates automatic decoding among average readers as well as struggling readers (Kuhn & Stahl, 2003). Furthermore, rereading can lead to improved comprehension (Chard et al., 2002). Poor readers who engage in repeated readings show marked improvement in speed, accuracy, and expression during oral rereading, and, more important, improvement is noted in reading comprehension.

Students need to become fluent or automatic in decoding to become skilled readers. After students have achieved some accuracy in word recognition, additional rereading enables them to become fluent. By exposing students to repeated reading, teachers help students become automatic decoders and thus good readers. Practicing oral reading fluency is an important reading component until the ninth grade (NICHD, 2000).

Implications for Whole-Group Reading Instruction

The practice of oral reading fluency in terms of whole-group instruction should be minimal. When the teacher reads aloud, students hear a fluent model, but that alone does not increase a student's oral reading fluency. The heterogeneous makeup of any classroom is typically comprised of a wide range of readers. Therefore, repeated readings of a grade-level text are of little benefit for those students reading either below or above grade level. Additionally, the whole-group setting does not allow for the individual feedback needed to improve oral reading fluency. Effective options for whole-group practice might include choral reading of poetry or short passages from text.

Implications for Small-Group Differentiated Reading Instruction

Fluency develops as a result of opportunities to practice reading with a high degree of success. In other words, fluency practice should be at an independent reading level where a student is reading with at least 98% accuracy. For struggling readers, the small-group format provides an opportunity to practice this important skill. Students in all small groups should reread text passages or even poetry at an independent reading level. Although the initial read of the text in the small-group setting is at the instructional level, the additional rereadings are at an independent reading level. This practice allows all readers to progress in their oral reading fluency and ultimately their overall reading comprehension.

Vocabulary

Vocabulary development is critical to reading development at all levels. In beginning reading, developing a basic sight word vocabulary is critical. As students mature and are capable of comprehending more complex text, vocabulary becomes the cornerstone of reading comprehension (Blachowicz & Fisher, 2000; Hennings, 2000). There are two types of vocabulary that are important to reading instruction: oral vocabulary and reading vocabulary. Oral vocabulary relates to words used in speaking or recognized in listening. Reading vocabulary refers to the words recognized or used in print. Vocabulary can be taught in two ways: indirectly and directly (NICHD, 2000). Indirect learning of vocabulary occurs when students hear and see words in many contexts, such as being read to, having conversations, or by students reading extensively on their own. Direct vocabulary instruction occurs when students are explicitly taught words or word-learning strategies.

Implications for Whole-Group Reading Instruction

Whole-group instruction provides fertile ground for the development of oral and listening vocabulary. Students begin to acquire oral vocabulary in their earliest school experiences. Many students come to school with a very limited oral vocabulary and need a language-rich classroom filled with words: words in stories, from conversations with adults and students, in rhymes, about the world around them, and so forth. It is impossible to overemphasize the importance of reading aloud to students of all ages, especially in a whole-group setting. In some instances, as students matriculate through the grades, teachers find less time to read to students. It is imperative that teachers continue to read above grade level in both fiction and nonfiction text to increase vocabulary. This preselected vocabulary should be taught in a systematic manner where words are pretaught, taught in context, and reviewed numerous times after they are read. In many cases, students who have passed the decoding stage in reading are limited in comprehension by their shear lack of "what words mean."

Implications for Small-Group Differentiated Reading Instruction

Small-group reading instruction is essential for initial reading vocabulary acquisition. Beginning readers must first master a basic sight word reading vocabulary before focusing on vocabulary that supports the text's message. Therefore, the small-group differentiated format adjusts vocabulary instruction based on the unique needs of the readers.

Vocabulary development can be best supported and enhanced as students explore text at appropriate instructional levels.

Comprehension

The real reason that we all learn to read is to comprehend the text's message. Research is clear that comprehension can be improved by helping readers use specific strategies (Block & Pressley, 2000). Comprehension strategies are sets of steps that good readers use to make sense of the text they are reading. The National Reading Panel report (NICHD, 2000) identified six strategies that have a firm research basis for improving text comprehension including monitoring, using graphic organizers, answering questions, generating questions, recognizing story structure, and summarizing. Teaching comprehension can be a formidable task, especially when students are still focusing on each word. At this point in reading development, comprehension should not be the primary focus. As students develop oral reading fluency, comprehension becomes more important. Research supports the fact that comprehension strategies can be and should be taught explicitly both in whole-group and small-group instruction (Harvey & Goudvis, 2002; NICHD).

Implications for Whole-Group Reading Instruction

There are two big jobs in reading: decoding and comprehension. To comprehend, a student must first pass through the decoding stage of reading development. Most kindergarten and first-grade students are in the decoding stage of reading development and, therefore, receive much of their comprehension instruction in terms of teacher read-alouds in a whole-group setting. Primary teachers can begin to build comprehension foundations with quality read-alouds well before students are able to read on their own. The reading process is long and laborious, and all beginning readers should be aware at an early stage that the ultimate goal of reading is comprehension. With so much to teach and so little time left of the instructional day, each read-aloud should include a comprehension strategy focus that is explicitly taught whether it be summarizing, recognizing cause-and-effect relationships, identifying story elements, questioning, and so forth. Beginning readers as well as advanced readers should be well aware that the ultimate goal of reading is to understand the text's message.

Implications for Small-Group Differentiated Reading Instruction

The reading process requires that readers progress through developmental stages. These beginning stages are focused on the decoding process with a gradual transition toward a comprehension focus. Therefore, the beginning stages of reading development have less emphasis on comprehension. Although the texts at this level are so simplistic that they require little skill to comprehend, teachers should have students complete simple predicting, summarizing, and questioning as these simple texts are explored. Comprehension for students in these early reading stages is best left to stories introduced during teacher read-alouds in whole-group instruction because these texts are typically more complex. As students progress to more advanced stages of reading development, comprehension becomes an important of the small-group instructional model and is taught explicitly.

What Makes the Small-Group Differentiated Reading Model Successful?

Models are representations that combine common parts into a whole. Models also suggest how the valued parts of a system might work together. Developing a model inclusive of differentiated reading stages and research-based components helps us to understand the reading process as a whole. Anchored in research, the Small-Group Differentiated Reading Model brings together many complex reading strategies. However, it is because the model has been systematically developed that the instructional components carry special weight. There are several aspects of this differentiated reading model that support its success.

- Small-group differentiated instruction provides systematic and comprehensive coverage of the strategies required to move students to greater achievement in reading.

- The teacher ensures that the reading activities are "respectful." Every group of students is given quality reading instruction and tasks that are worthwhile, valuable, and matched to students' instructional level.

- Assessment is ongoing and directly linked to instruction. Students are regularly assessed on fluency, instructional reading, and word study levels. Teachers gather information from both formal and informal assessments about how their students are progressing in their learning at any given point. Whatever the teacher can glean about student reading readiness helps the teacher plan the next steps in reading instruction.

- Students are constantly evaluated, shuffled, and reshuffled in flexible groups to best meet instructional needs.

- Small-group differentiated reading provides intensive and continually adjusted instruction in fluency, word study, vocabulary, and comprehension.

- Differentiated reading takes into consideration the individual characteristics of the children, capitalizes on the strengths they have, and expands and challenges their abilities.

- The individual components of the Small-Group Differentiated Reading Model work interactively, building on and supporting one another. Each lesson introduces a new book or new piece of text. The rereading of this book builds sight word vocabulary, promotes strategy use, and increases fluency. In addition, new words for the vocabulary word bank are selected from the new reading selections. The sentence writing includes words taken from the word bank as well as from the word study. Comprehension is focused on the text being read in group, and written responses often include story vocabulary. Therefore, this model allows for the interactive development of reading, word study, vocabulary, and comprehension.

- Each lesson is based on best reading research–based practices and includes all components identified as important to reading success.

Implications for ELLs, Special Needs Students, and Intervention

Perhaps the most important reason that the Small-Group Differentiated Reading Model is successful is its ability to meet the needs of a wide range of readers. Teachers continue to be challenged with readers who struggle and those who have special needs, including students who do not speak English. As these teachers more thoroughly understand the stages of reading development, they feel better equipped to meet the needs of these challenges.

ELLs who have a good English listening vocabulary are often easy to place in the Small-Group Differentiated Reading Model because the model already allows for differences among learners. Of course ELLs (and often students with low socioeconomic background) lack the vocabulary or background knowledge of some of their peers. Teachers need to spend extra time developing the background and vocabulary necessary for good comprehension. This is easier to do when using a model that places students at their instructional reading level and word study level.

ELLs with limited English lack the oral vocabulary needed to support their decoding and comprehension efforts. I have found that selecting books with good text and picture correlation supports vocabulary development in ELLs in much the same way that it supports decoding in beginning reading. Without this crucial ingredient, ELLs become nonsense decoders who have little hope of comprehending all that they read. Beginning with simple texts also allows students to develop a sense of predictable sentence structure critical to the ELLs. Small-group differentiated reading instruction provides the components that ELLs need to be successful readers.

Additional reading intervention outside of the literacy block is important to those students performing below expectations. New federal guidelines in the RTI model suggest that early intervention for struggling students be delivered in an explicit and consistent manner outside of the literacy block. A prevalent model for delivery of primary reading instruction and intervention is called the three-tier reading model. This three-tier model is an attempt to prevent reading failure through early intervention rather than testing and placing students into special education. It consists of three levels of instruction: Tier I is the basic reading instruction delivered in the literacy block, Tier II is reading intervention that takes place outside of the literacy block, and Tier III provides additional intense reading instruction for students who continue to struggle. The Small-Group Differentiated Reading Model plays a key role in each of these levels of reading instruction because of its ability to adjust to the needs of the individual student.

Students identified as those with special needs or who require more reading assistance have often been assigned to a "different" reading program or boxed program, with the hope that the program would be more effective in meeting their needs. This model has, for the most part, allowed these students to fall further behind because of the lack of differentiated strategies in scripted programs. The days of sending the special needs students down the hall for the literacy block are quickly coming to an end. The new RTI model supports a reading model for regular classroom reading instruction along with intervention. In other words, a model that supports *additional* instruction, not one that replaces regular reading instruction. Realistically, what these students need is more appropriate instruction geared to their instructional reading and word study level delivered in a more intense format. Using the Small-Group Differentiated Reading Model for reading intervention provides the intensity that these students require. Teachers also recognize that their knowledge about the teaching of reading will best prepare them to meet the needs of students with special needs.

Components in a Balanced Literacy Model: Literacy Venues

Although this book focuses on small-group differentiated reading instruction and its importance, the additional components of a balanced literacy program cannot be overlooked (see Figure 2). During the school day, reading and writing instruction is delivered in either whole group, small group, or independent practice. In whole group, literacy instruction is delivered through teacher modeling or a shared instructional format. It is, therefore, important to examine the research-based reading practices best taught and practiced in these settings. In essence, these are the delivery systems or venues we use to teach literacy. Small-group differentiated reading is a critical part of balanced literacy instruction, which, when implemented effectively, gives every student the opportunity to become a successful reader.

Modeled Reading (Read-Aloud)

Reading aloud to students plays a critical role in literacy development. This format allows the teacher to read above the reading level of most of the students in the classroom and therefore provides a rich format for a wide range of learners. Reading aloud allows children to connect to the text and experience the excitement and pleasure in reading. Additionally, teacher read-aloud is a powerful tool for teaching explicit listening comprehension and listening vocabulary to children who are beginning the reading process.

For the first time in my career in education, early childhood teachers have told me that they are frustrated by a lack of motivation in some students to want to learn to read. When I was a teacher of young children, I found that most students could hardly wait to come to school to learn to read. However, now many students simply lack experiences in hearing great stories traditionally read at home. In most households, both parents work and in some cases have more than one job so students don't have as many opportunities to be read to at home. As students enter school, their motivation to become a reader occurs in two ways. First, as teachers read aloud to students to share the joy of reading, students are motivated to want to learn to read and read more. Second, an overlooked yet critical motivator is giving students books that they can read successfully. One student recently told me, "Success feels good." That statement pretty much says it all. Students who are routinely given books to read at a frustration level will soon lose motivation. Students get excited about reading when they are surrounded by a variety of books to explore, read, and enjoy. It is, therefore, the teacher's responsibility to provide a literacy-rich

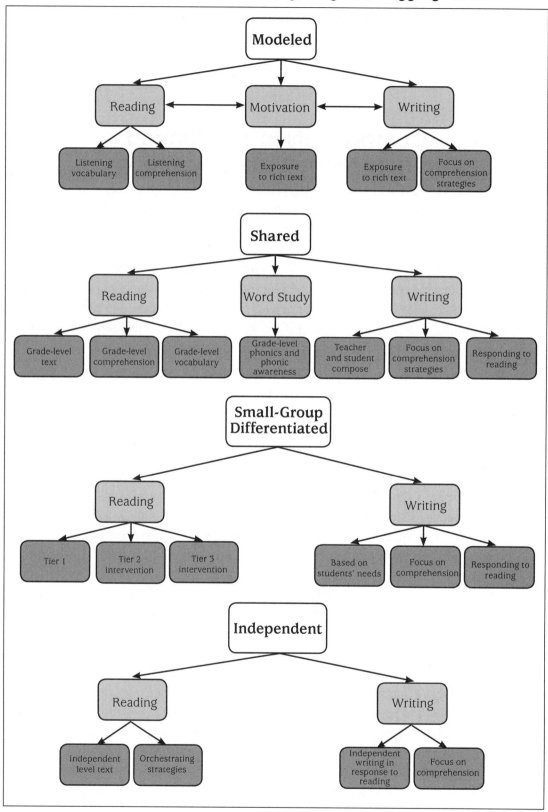

environment. Children come to school expecting to learn to read. It is only when we fail to support these readers in meaningful ways that motivation becomes an issue.

Modeled Writing

Modeled writing provides teachers with the opportunity to demonstrate the thinking processes of a writer as he or she responds to a text. With a particular comprehension strategy as a focus, the teacher uses think-aloud strategies as he or she composes the text's message. This provides students with an opportunity to observe the comprehension process with a deeper understanding of the text communicated in writing. Formats for the modeled writing might include the use of graphic organizers, charts, lists, or short written pieces. One way that teachers can always attract a focused audience for modeled writing is by making personal connections with the text as they write about the text. Children find it refreshing that teachers do have a life outside of the classroom. Modeled writing also can serve as a venue for demonstrating writing processes.

Shared Reading

Shared reading is perhaps the most misunderstood venue as it relates to balanced literacy. The primary focus for shared reading is to share grade-level text; therefore, the teacher is primarily responsible for reading the text. Shared reading pieces are generally written at grade level with each student having access to the text. Although the teacher is primarily responsible for reading the text, he or she actively engages the students as they follow along in the text or participate with the teacher in choral reading. Choral reading provides the support necessary to give all students access to the text. Major focuses in shared reading instruction are explicit teaching of grade-level vocabulary and comprehension strategies. Shared reading can also be used as a strategy to read grade-level text in the content areas. The shared reading venue supports readers as they access grade-level texts and standards.

Note that calling on individual students during shared reading should be avoided because it is not an effective strategy. If the primary focus is comprehension, for example, and if the story is read by multiple readers—some fluent, some struggling—it is difficult at best to comprehend the text's message. Another way that teachers routinely share the weekly story is by playing a taped version. However, this is not an effective or appropriate strategy for whole-group instruction. By using a taped version of the text, many comprehension opportunities are relinquished. As the teacher reads the story while the students follow along or perhaps whisper read with the teacher, the text becomes the framework for rich conversation, questioning, and exploring the text more deeply. Another common practice in many classrooms is to reread the story several times during the week. Again, this strategy must be more closely examined. Many teachers feel stressed that their students must pass the weekly test based on the story; therefore, they read the stories numerous times. Unfortunately, the students may become better at listening but not reading. This is especially true for struggling readers where the grade-level text is too hard. For average or advanced readers, a maximum of two reads should be considered. This would also allow for students to read more books and ultimately get better at reading. We have already established that whole group is not an efficient way to practice fluency. Teachers should always ask themselves, What is my purpose in this activity? In reading instruction, the answer should be one of the research-based components: fluency, phonics, phonemic awareness, vocabulary, or comprehension.

Shared Writing

In much the same way that shared reading support readers, shared writing supports writers as the teacher and students compose the text's message together. With the teacher acting as scribe, students respond to a commonly shared text focusing on a specific comprehension strategy. Although comprehension is the intended objective, this venue also provides a rich format for teaching the writing process as well as standard conventions of writing. The literacy block dictates that the writing process not be taught during this time frame, but when combined with a comprehension focus, the two work well together. Writing encourages a deeper understanding of the text's message. The ultimate goal is for students to be able to express their understanding of the reading through writing.

Small-Group Differentiated Reading

Small-group differentiated reading instruction is a critical component of the balanced reading model. The small-group model should be used both for primary instruction in the literacy block as well as for reading intervention. The primary classroom can be a place of great diversity. Students can be diverse in their instructional reading and word study levels as well as the time and instructional setting that is required for them to succeed. Because students progress at different rates, it is important to have structures in place (other than special services) that provide for an immediate response to their needs through additional intervention. This format works well for the regular classroom teachers as well as in intervention models such as the three-tier reading model and RTI discussed earlier in this chapter. Students who struggle need more time in a smaller instructional group and not necessarily a different program.

Small-Group Differentiated Writing

The writing process develops in stages much like beginning reading. Therefore, the small-group setting provides writers with an opportunity to receive instruction geared to the group's needs. Writing is a skill that must be modeled, supported, and practiced. Differentiated writing instruction brings together writers with like needs so that teachers are better equipped to deliver appropriate instruction. When the writing in small group supports or is an extension of reading, comprehension also increases. Research is clear that writing instruction can raise reading achievement (Tierney & Shanahan, 1991). Many classroom models require that writing be taught outside the reading block. When comprehension is the focus of the writing activity, writing can most certainly be included as a part of the reading block. Furthermore, writing and reading are so innately entwined that they support and build upon one another.

Independent Reading and Writing

Finally, "practice makes perfect" is a phrase that we need to pay closer attention to as teachers. Students get better at reading and writing by practicing these skills at appropriate independent levels. This important piece of a balanced reading program should take place while small-group reading groups are being conducted. The days of "drop everything and read" are quickly coming to an end. With an ever-shrinking instructional day, this activity should take place while the teacher is working in small group. In my opinion, teachers are often overly stressed about what the other students are doing during small-group instruction. When implemented most effectively, the activities that students are engaged in are extensions of the work done in small group. For example, students who have completed reading a book in group might be asked to reread the book with a partner outside of group to practice fluency. Or, a group studying common *a* vowel patterns might be assigned a word hunt where they find words in books that have the same vowel patterns. Teachers need to ensure that they do not assign tasks to the rest of the class that are not at appropriate independent reading, word study, or writing levels. Students become frustrated, management problems surface, and off-task behavior is exhibited. Simply put, students need to be doing more reading or listening to reading, writing in response to reading, and working with words. Careful planning for independent reading and writing activities promotes quality time spent away from the direct supervision of the teacher. (See Chapter 9 for more information on this topic.)

Organizing and Managing the Literacy Block: Whole-Group, Small-Group, and Independent Practice

The challenge in orchestrating the literacy block, which consists of whole-group, small-group, and independent reading, can be best described as putting together a literacy jigsaw puzzle. Consideration must be given to grade-level literacy standards, reading research–based components, and the developmental reading and word study levels of all students. In most instances, the literacy block is no less than 90–120 minutes of focused instruction.

Table 3 depicts the literacy block and the components that should be included in an effective delivery model (a discussion of the balanced literacy model, which provides the framework for the literacy block, was discussed in the previous section). The literacy block comprises the core reading program based on scientific research and grade-level standards which may include the basal or alternate grade-level reading curriculum, small-group differentiated reading, and independent literacy activities. The literacy block addresses all five components of reading research in both whole-group and small-group instruction: (1) oral reading fluency, (2) comprehension, (3) phonemic awareness (where appropriate), (4) vocabulary, and (5) comprehension. In whole-group instruction, these elements are addressed in terms of grade-level standards. In a similar way, small-group instruction addresses the same research-based components but at the developmental

TABLE 3
The Literacy Block

Time	Curriculum	Instructional Venue	Text
10–15 minutes	Quality fiction and nonfiction text Focus: Listening vocabulary Listening comprehension	Modeled Reading (Teacher Read-Aloud) Whole group	Above grade-level text
30–45 minutes	Basal Program or Grade-level Alternative Focus: Grade-level literacy standards	Shared Reading Whole group Cooperative groups	Grade-level text
20–30 minutes x number of small groups	Small-Group Differentiated Reading Model Focus: Fluency Developmental word study Vocabulary Comprehension	Small group (6 or fewer students)	Instructional reading level
30+ minutes	Independent Reading Independent practice of key components	Individuals or partners	Independent reading level

levels of the students and the differentiated materials that are required. A common misunderstanding among teachers is that small-group instruction is primarily for at-risk students. On the contrary, small-group instruction is for all students, although the struggling readers might be seen more frequently. Based on my experience, a good offense is a great defense: Providing quality instruction in the regular classroom setting during the literacy block is the most powerful way to prevent reading failure.

Perhaps the biggest obstacle in implementing this literacy model is time management. If the literacy block is shorter, consider completing the read-aloud component outside of the block and choose a book that supports standards in social studies or science. If a basal program is the centerpiece of whole-group grade-level instruction, choose the activities carefully. In some instances, not all activities included are powerful or even make sense for the readers in your classroom. By picking and choosing wisely, time will be freed up to do the things that are the most important as well as motivating to students.

A Look Ahead

Chapter 2 begins with an in-depth look at each of the reading research–based components and the strategies and activities that support each stage of the Small-Group Differentiated Reading Model. These components include fluency (rereading), vocabulary, (word bank) word study (phonemic awareness, phonics, and common word features), and comprehension.

Chapter 3 discusses the assessments that support the Small-Group Differentiated Reading Model. The Early Reading Screening Instrument (ERSI) provides an initial assessment for nonreaders. Using information gained through the ERSI allows teachers to make informed decisions as they assign prereaders for small-group instruction based on individual literacy needs. As students' literacy levels increase, additional assessments are provided to help teachers continue to track students' progress. These assessments provide important information concerning word study levels, sight word knowledge, and instructional reading levels to maximize learning opportunities. These assessments also provide valuable information for curriculum planning, student groupings, and individual growth.

Chapters 4 through 8 are structured similarly and present the five stages of early reading development. In each chapter, a brief review of student characteristics associated with each specific reading stage is presented followed by appropriate text recommendations. A lesson plan format that supports each developmental stage also is included in each of these chapters. Step-by-step directions are given for implementing the lesson plan, followed by selected teacher and student dialogue that supports the lesson. This dialogue is included to demonstrate the activities in an authentic small-group setting; all student names are pseudonyms. Independent Activity Alerts are interspersed throughout these chapters to provide suggestions for easy-to-implement activities that are appropriate for each stage of reading development.

Chapter 9 discusses how to engage and manage students while the teacher is conducting small-group instruction. Activities that support the reading research–based components and that focus on the developmental reading and word study levels of students are suggested. These activities are both easy to implement as well as powerful in providing independent practice. Responsibility sheets that coordinate with student developmental levels are also included.

The accompanying CD contains essential information concerning assessments and materials necessary to implement the Small-Group Differentiated Reading Model. Table 4 shows the contents listing for the CD. These materials are referred to throughout the book and can be located solely on the CD.

TABLE 4
Contents Listing for Accompanying CD

Assessment Materials	Early Reading Screening Instrument
	Reading Review
	Spelling Assessments
	    Stage 1: Alphabet Production
	    Stage 2A: Initial Consonant Sounds
	    Stage 2B: Initial Consonant Blends/Digraphs
	    Stage 3A: Word Families
	    Stage 3B: Short Vowels
	    Stage 4: Vowel Patterns 1
	    Stage 5A: Vowel Patterns 2
	    Stage 5B: Common Word Features
	Oral Reading Fluency Rating Scales
	    Grade 1
	    Grade 2
	    Grade 3
	Sight Word Assessment
	Student Reading Assessment Profile Sheet
	Classroom Profile Sheet

Word Study Materials	Emergent Reader
	    Word Study Scope and Sequence (Alphabet Recognition and Production)
	    100 Most Frequent Words in Books for Beginning Readers
	    Letter Cards
	    Sight Word Cards
	    Cut-Up Sentences
	Beginning Reader
	    Word Study Scope and Sequence (Initial Consonant Sounds, Digraphs, and Blends)
	    Picture Cards
	    Cut-Up Sentences
	Fledgling Reader
	    Word Study Scope and Sequence (Word Families and Short Vowels)
	    Word Study Cards (Word Families and Short Vowels)
	    Elkonin Boxes (3 boxes)
	    Elkonin Boxes (4 boxes)
	    Spelling Sort (3 boxes)
	    Spelling Sort (4 boxes)
	    Word Ladders
	    Word Scramble Activities
	    Dictated Sentences
	Transitional Reader
	    Word Study Scope and Sequence (Vowel Patterns 1)
	    Word Study Cards (Vowel Patterns 1)
	    Make and Write (Word Scramble)
	    Word Scramble Activities
	    Dictated Sentences
	Independent Reader
	    Word Study Scope and Sequence (Vowel Patterns 2 and Common Word Features)
	    Word Study Cards (Vowel Patterns 2 and Common Word Features)
	    Word Scramble Activities
	    Dictated Sentences

(continued)

TABLE 4
Contents Listing for Accompanying CD (continued)

Auxiliary Instructional Materials	Beat the Clock
	Buddy Reading Log
	Cause and Effect
	Circle Story
	Compare/Contrast
	Cut-Up Sentence Template
	First, Then, Next, Finally
	Listening Center Log
	Main Ideas/Details
	Memory
	Reading Lesson Plans
	Emergent Reader (Stage 1)
	Beginning Reader (Stage 2)
	Fledgling Reader (Stage 3)
	Transitional Reader (Stage 4)
	Independent Reader (Stage 5)
	Reading Log
	Record and Reflect
	Story Map
	Summarize With Vocabulary
	The Top Five Things About…
	Vocabulary Map
	Watch Our Sight Words Grow
	Weekly Responsibility Sheet for Stage 1: Emergent Readers
	Weekly Responsibility Sheet for Stage 2: Beginning Readers
	Weekly Responsibility Sheet for Stages 3, 4, and 5: Fledgling, Transitional, and Independent Readers
	Word Hunt
	Word Study Card Template
	Word Wizard Cards

Instructional Strategies and Activities in the Small-Group Differentiated Reading Model

The power of the Small-Group Differentiated Reading Model lies in the strong research base of its components, strategies, and activities. It is important here to clearly define the terms *strategies, components,* and *activities*. A *strategy* is a tool that helps a reader effectively address one of the five reading research–based *components*: fluency, vocabulary, phonemic awareness, phonics, and comprehension. For example, if the component being addressed in the model is comprehension, the strategies might include summarizing the text, recognizing main ideas and details, or questioning. An *activity* to support summarizing might be retelling. On the other hand if the focus is fluency, the strategy might be rereading and a specific activity to practice rereading might be choral reading. Carefully devised lesson plans provide differentiated instruction that supports the reading research–based components of fluency, vocabulary, phonemic awareness, phonics, and comprehension as students progress through the first five stages of reading development. The lesson plans that support this model provide both the strategies and activities that address these components in a supportive and meaningful way. Although specific steps for implementing the model will be discussed in Chapters 4 through 8, it is important to examine the strategies and activities that support the components as well as their importance to the stages of reading development.

Fluency (Rereading)

To acquire oral reading fluency, students must have enough guided practice for reading to become automatic; therefore, rereading is the key to building oral reading fluency. Oral reading fluency is achieved as students learn to read quickly, accurately, and with enough expression to understand the text's message. There is strong evidence to support that students who spend a lot of time reading become good readers (Farstrup & Samuels, 2002). The new read portion of the lesson plan allows students to explore a new text daily in a supported environment where feedback encourages growth, and the rereading provides the practice to build fluency.

Reading and rereading books are consistent strategies in building fluency in each stage of the Small-Group Differentiated Reading Model. Beginning readers can become disillusioned with the reading process if they do not actually have a book in their hands and are therefore given books to read in the first stage. The Emergent Reader stage (Stage

1) begins with books using repetitive text and pictures to tell the story, also known as high picture support. The focus of these strategies in this stage is to have extended practice in tracking print and using picture clues. This is the skill that must be acquired before oral reading fluency can be addressed. The Beginning Reader stage (Stage 2) builds on this process by advancing to text that is less repetitive and has more words on a page. By this time, students are also practicing their decoding skills, which include the knowledge of using beginning and ending sounds and recognizing some sight words. Although still in the developing stages, oral reading fluency is being formed as students practice automaticity in recognizing words quickly and accurately. The need for rereading in each subsequent stage now focuses on the development of oral reading fluency. As students continue to build fluency in the Transitional Reader stage (Stage 4), the text becomes more complex and therefore the speed, accuracy, and expression are critical to the comprehension process. The Independent Reader stage (Stage 5) marks a milestone in the reading process in which students have developed the decoding skills and contextual knowledge necessary to become independent readers (basically capable of reading text at the mid-to-late second-grade level). Although these readers continue to practice fluency, this can be accomplished by reading and rereading a short selection such as a poem or a passage from the text.

Whereas other small-group reading models do not encourage individual oral reading by students, this Small-Group Differentiated Reading Model embraces oral reading as an important strategy. The National Reading Panel report (NICHD, 2000) points out that guided oral reading with teacher feedback has a significant positive impact on word recognition, reading fluency, and comprehension. In fact, the report further states that guided oral reading benefits both poor and good readers at least through fourth grade. Conversely, the report was unable to determine if silent reading improves fluency. The Small-Group Differentiated Reading Model includes oral reading as students read and reread a variety of texts.

Frequent opportunities to read aloud make sense for beginning readers. First, oral reading helps connect children with experiences they have had at home, preschools, or kindergartens where adults have read to them (Neuman & Dickinson, 2002). In addition, oral reading gives teachers observable characteristics of an otherwise unobservable process. This provides teachers with a means for checking progress, diagnosing problems, and focusing instruction. Ultimately, oral reading provides an opportunity for young readers to share their emerging abilities with their peers, parents, and teachers.

As with many reading strategies, traditional round-robin reading in which students take turns reading orally has been deemed a poor strategy because of its misuse. This misuse stems from practices that forced students to read instructionally inappropriate text and included an unequal distribution of turns. However, this technique has some benefits when used appropriately and sparingly with instructional- or independent-level text. Research shows that children reading aloud and receiving instruction from the teacher get far more instructional feedback than the students following along (Kuhn & Stahl, 2003).

Opportunities to read aloud and listen to others read are parts of a total literacy community. When teachers read aloud, it whets children's appetite. Similarly, oral reading, when done appropriately, builds self-confidence and a desire to share good stories with others. What follows is a discussion of activities that provide students with multiple opportunities to reread orally.

Activities That Support Oral Reading Fluency in the Small-Group Reading Model

Rereading is arguably the most important strategy in developing oral reading fluency. There are numerous activities that are useful as students reread the text to develop fluency. Varying these activities keep students actively engaged and motivated as they practice this important skill.

Choral Reading: In this activity, the group reads and rereads the whole text or part of the text in unison, led by the teacher. This technique is especially useful for emergent and beginning readers because it allows students to have multiple opportunities to read the text with teacher and peer support. Choral reading is an excellent way to read a new text because of the teacher support provided.

Stop and Go Reading: This is a modified version of choral reading. As the teacher and students choral read, the teacher stops and allows the students to continue. As needed, the teacher may rejoin the group to assist with fluency, speed, or expression. This activity builds reading stamina, allowing the students to carry the responsibility of reading the text without complete teacher support.

Lead Reading: This technique is especially useful for rereading text. In lead reading, one student is the leader and reads aloud the text while the other students in the group whisper read along with the lead reader. New readers love to share their new reading skills, and this gives them an opportunity to do so while engaging the other students at the same time. Additionally, this gives the teacher an opportunity to informally assess individual reading fluency.

Whisper Reading: Whisper reading is effective when used as a rereading technique. In this activity, each student whisper reads the text at his or her own speed. This allows each student to reread the entire text to build fluency. While the students whisper read, the teacher "listens in" on individual students. A "reading telephone" made from PVC pipe allows students to reread without the distraction of hearing other readers. Additionally, the teacher can set a timer for 3–4 minutes and have the students stop whisper reading when the timer goes off. This strategy accommodates students who read at various speeds without wasting valuable small-group instructional time. Another way to use whisper reading is with more fluent readers. Students are asked to whisper read a short section of the text for a purpose. For example, the teacher might say, "Let's all whisper read the next page to find out what John did to solve the problem." This encourages some reading independence with teacher support.

Partner Reading: Each student is paired with another student in the small-group setting. The two students take turns reading previously read text. One student reads while the other student gives assistance and feedback. Then, the process is reversed. The teacher monitors by listening in on the reading pairs, assisting when necessary. In addition, partner reading outside of group with a book previously read in group is an excellent way to practice fluency.

Echo Reading: This strategy is especially useful for emergent readers who are learning to track print. In this activity, the teacher reads the page first while the students follow along. Then, the students read chorally with the teacher. Echo reading also is useful when the teacher models oral reading fluency.

Individual Student Reading: As previously stated, asking individual students to read in the small group can be used occasionally, especially as teachers need to complete informal oral reading assessments. Keep the passages short, and require the other students to follow along to keep all readers engaged.

Word Study (Phonemic Awareness, Phonics, Word Features)

The goal in word study is to provide young readers with the knowledge to give them effortless recognition of words. Word study is not an instructional program but an instructional process. This differentiated word study model provides teachers with a routine for presenting lessons to students in an effective compare-and-contrast strategy. Although there are no phonics rules to be memorized, children are encouraged to discover spelling patterns in the language. The strategies that support word study including sorting, writing, and practicing automaticity.

Sorting teaches students how to recognize patterns in words, not just how to sound out words. Conversely, many traditional phonics programs encourage students to see words in parts, which hinders the learning process by asking students to sound out each letter. The word sort approach used in this model allows children to develop accuracy without the use of workbooks or ditto sheets. Activities that support sorting include games that are short, challenging, and engaging.

This small-group model includes writing as a strategy that supports word study. Students have the opportunity to apply their word study skills through activities such as cut-up sentences and sentence dictations. When taught appropriately, the processes of developmental reading and writing go hand in hand. In the Small-Group Differentiated Reading Model, sentences geared to a group's word study level provide the material for a writing experience. Written texts demonstrate standard form and spelling for young writers. For example, for reading groups working in the Emergent and Beginning Reading stages of the small-group model, the teacher acts as scribe in the writing experience. The sentence would include some words that contain the focused beginning sounds as well as some sight words. The teacher writes the sentence on a sentence strip, cuts the words in the sentence apart, and asks the students to assist in reconstructing the sentence. This allows students to use strategies such as looking at beginning sounds in words, noticing capital letters, and recognizing high-frequency words. After the students have developed the skills necessary to write a sentence independently, the sentence-strip sequence is dropped. At this point, a sentence is dictated by the teacher, and the students write it independently. Linking reading and writing encourages students to practice known strategies that build confidence.

Automaticity is an important strategy as students build their fluency skills. The ultimate goal in word study is for students to quickly recognize patterns in words for decoding and comprehension. Activities that support automaticity are presented in game-like formats both in small group and in independent practice.

Much of the word study sequence in the Small-Group Differentiated Reading Model is adapted from Morris's (1999) *The Howard Street Tutoring Manual: Teaching At-Risk Readers in the Primary Grades*. Each word study lesson begins with a sorting activity with either alphabet letters, picture cards, or with students sorting word cards based on patterns. Sorting is a powerful strategy used for supporting word study skills. Based on my observations, word study begins as students become confident in alphabet recognition and production. In the Emergent Reader stage, students sort and match upper- and lowercase letters. When they master at least half of the alphabet, the students complete the alphabet study while concurrently developing phonemic awareness in hearing and identifying beginning consonant sounds. Students sort picture cards that represent words that have the focus beginning consonant sounds. In the Fledgling Reader stage, the lessons then progress sequentially through short-vowel word families and one-syllable, short-vowel words. The phonics sequence then turns to the study of common vowel patterns in the Transitional Reader stage. Finally, the Independent Reader stage begins with the study of less common vowel patterns. Word study concludes after the completion of less common vowel patterns in this stage with a focus on common word features including prefixes, suffixes, contractions, compound words, and homophones, which are useful for students reading at late first-, second-, and third-grade levels. The word study sequence is shown in Table 5.

In my experience, traditional reading instruction often ignores the significant relationship between word study and a student's reading level. A child should never be expected to spell a word that he or she cannot read. In the Small-Group Differentiated Reading Model, spelling is included as a part of word study and is developed incrementally with a child's reading level. See CD 💿 for word study materials including a word study scope and sequence for each stage of development and for the accompanying spelling assessments that are important in assessing students' word study knowledge as well as in tracking their progress.

Activities That Support Word Study in the Small-Group Reading Model

The following word study activities support students as they compare and contrast patterns in words. Both card sorts and spelling sorts help students solidify this foundational word knowledge. Additional activities support automaticity in recognizing and applying these patterns in reading and writing. See the accompanying CD 💿 for word study materials that correspond to these activities such as sample cut-up sentences and dictated sentences.

Card Sorting: There are two different kinds of word sorts: closed and open. In an open sort, the teacher gives the students explicit instructions about the word study features

TABLE 5
Word Study Sequence

1. Alphabet Recognition (upper- and lowercase)

2. Consonants (beginning)/Consonant Blends and Digraphs

3. Short-Vowel Word Families

1	2	3	4	5
a	i	o	u	e
-at	-it	-ot	-ut	-et
-an	-ig	-op	-ug	-ed
-ap	-in	-ob	-un	-en
-ack	-ick	-ock	-uck	-ell

4. Short Vowels

a	i	o	u	e
b<u>a</u>d	p<u>i</u>g	m<u>o</u>m	b<u>u</u>s	p<u>e</u>t

5. Vowel Patterns—Level 1

a	i	o	u	e
c<u>at</u>	h<u>i</u>d	m<u>o</u>m	m<u>u</u>d	r<u>e</u>d
m<u>a</u>ke	r<u>i</u>de	r<u>o</u>pe	c<u>u</u>te	f<u>ee</u>t
c<u>ar</u>	g<u>ir</u>l	f<u>or</u>	h<u>ur</u>t	h<u>er</u>
d<u>ay</u>		g<u>o</u>	bl<u>ue</u>	h<u>e</u>
		b<u>oa</u>t		
		l<u>oo</u>k		
		c<u>ow</u>		

6. Vowel Patterns—Level 2

a	i	o	u	e
r<u>ai</u>n	r<u>i</u>ght	t<u>o</u>ld		m<u>ea</u>t
b<u>a</u>ll	b<u>y</u>	m<u>oo</u>n		h<u>ea</u>d
s<u>aw</u>	f<u>i</u>nd	b<u>oi</u>l		n<u>ew</u>
		l<u>ow</u>		
		l<u>ou</u>d		
		b<u>oy</u>		

(continued)

TABLE 5
Word Study Sequence (continued)

7. Common Word Features

Contractions	Prefixes	Suffixes (plurals)	Compound Words	Homophones (examples)
is	pre	s	night	ate/eight
not	re	es	any	hall/haul
had	un	y/i/add es	every	by/buy/bye
would				their/there/they're
are				plane/plain
have				hair/hare

and gives examples with the header cards that establish the pattern. For example, the header card for an āCe word (long *a*, consonant, *e*) could be *made*. Students then sort the words based on the patterns established by the header cards. An open sort gives students the opportunity to sort the cards without specific instruction by the teacher regarding the word features; this process allows students to use critical thinking skills to discover patterns in words. Card sorting can take place in small groups and in independent practice.

Spelling Sort: This type of sort is critical in solidifying students' abilities to recognize and reproduce the patterns being studied. This activity can be used for word study beginning with short-vowel families and in all of the subsequent word study lessons. Students write the focus patterns or "header words" in the boxes at the top of the page. The teacher then calls out words containing the featured patterns. The students visually sort based on the pattern and write the word under the correct pattern. See CD 💿 for Spelling Sort templates for three and four patterns.

Word Scramble: Using a hands-on approach, students physically move letters around in this activity to form and re-form words based on the patterns being studied. This activity is powerful as students make connections with patterns in words. See CD 💿 for Word Scramble activities that accompany each word study sequence and a template for the activity Make and Write, which provides an opportunity for students to complete the word scramble using the moveable letters and then write the words.

Word Ladders: Using the Words Scramble activities (again, see CD 💿), students write the words instead of making them with moveable letters. This activity begins as students write the first word at the top of a ladder (either on notebook paper or using the reproducible form on the CD). For example, the teacher can ask students to write the word *make*. Directly under the word, the next step might be to drop one letter and add two letters to make the word *shake*. The process continues as students write the next words vertically on the ladder.

Cut-Up Sentences: This activity is used in the first two stages: Emergent and Beginning readers. The teacher acts as scribe as a sentence that contains focuses from the word study is written on a sentence strip. For example, if a group of beginning readers is studying the beginning sounds *b*, *s*, and *m*, the cut-up sentence might be "The soft bunny is mine." This sentence contains words with the focus sounds, along with some basic sight words. When the sentence is completed with the students' contributions, the teacher cuts apart the sentence and gives each student a piece of the sentence. The sentence is then put back together. This activity also reinforces concept of word and sight word recognition.

Dictated Sentences: Dictated sentences are used to ensure that students can make the transition from sorting the words and spelling them in isolation to applying this skill in the context of a sentence. This also assists students in solidifying word meanings.

Memory: Teachers can teach students to play this game in group and then use it primarily as an independent follow-up activity after the first two stages have been completed. Using the focus alphabet letters, picture cards, or word pattern cards, the teacher turns sets of the cards over (four or five pairs). Students then take turns making appropriate matches with upper- and lowercase letters, picture cards that have the same beginning sounds, or words that contain the same patterns. Using this activity in the small-group model is not always an efficient use of time because students must wait for a turn. An alternative to using this strategy is to have pairs of students complete the game rather than playing one game with the entire group.

Speed Drills: Speed drills are an important independent activity as students develop the ability to recognize common patterns in words with automaticity. The teacher selects several word study cards from each of the focus patterns, shuffles them, and then places them in a deck of cards. Using the Word Wizard game format (discussed later in this chapter) the students identify the words cards as quickly as possible.

Vocabulary (Word Bank)

Instruction in reading vocabulary is first grounded in the study of sight words seen most frequently in beginning readers. Whereas sight words are most often taught in the classroom using word walls, this customized word bank is an important strategy used as a vehicle to increase automaticity in sight word recognition in the first three stages of the Small-Group Differentiated Reading Model. Following the sequential list of 100 Most Frequent Words in Books for Beginning Readers (see CD for this list in the word study materials section), the vocabulary word bank for Emergent Readers begins by building a bank of the first 15 sight words. These words are frequently found in the books being read and reread in the small group that helps establish a connection between the word bank and the words seen in text. This word bank grows gradually and is reviewed in each lesson to enhance automaticity in word recognition. During the Beginning Reading stage, the process simply continues as the teacher adds new words to the bank and students generally work toward mastery of the first 50 sight words. It is important to note that the word bank should never contain more than 20–25 words at one time, because there won't be enough time in the small-group lesson to accommodate numerous words. So, for example, when students automatically recognize the first 25 words on the list, drop the five words they know best and add the next five words to the list. In the Fledgling Reader stage, the group generally finishes up with the 100 sight words and the focus then turns to story vocabulary that is important to the understanding of the text.

In Stages 4 and 5, the word bank continues to support vocabulary development as students begin to read across a variety of genres. The teacher preselects words that are important to the meaning of the text to preview before reading. During the reading, these words are reviewed in terms of the context. After reading, the vocabulary is revisited to summarize the text. Additionally, common words that the group continues to miss can also be housed in the vocabulary word bank.

Activities That Support Vocabulary Development in the Small-Group Reading Model

The activities that support vocabulary development include a focus on developing automaticity in recognizing sight words. In addition, focusing on the meaning of words in context becomes an important part of comprehension as students read more complex text. See the accompanying CD for auxiliary instructional materials that correspond to these activities.

Word Wizard: During the first three stages of reading development, this word card game encourages student automaticity in recognizing sight words. The game begins with the teacher reviewing the word bank words on cards with the entire group. Then, the teacher sets a timer for 1–2 minutes. The teacher then flashes one word at a time to individual students. If a student recognizes the word, he or she keeps it. If a student does not recognize the word in 3 seconds, the teacher shows the word to the next student. Include the following word cards in the word bank, too: pass, reverse, skip, or zap (this card means that the player must give all of his or her cards back). These cards make the game more exciting for the students. When the timer goes off, the player with the most cards wins. (Word Wizard cards can be found on the CD .)

Vocabulary Maps: Vocabulary maps can be modeled in group and then used as an extension activity. Generally, vocabulary maps help students focus on one word and describe it in terms of what it looks like, what it means, how to use it in the context of a sentence, or give a synonym or antonym for it.

Picture This: Students draw visual representations of vocabulary words. Using a piece of plain paper folded into four squares, students use each box to illustrate a word. This activity can be completed both in and out of the group. Additionally, these pictures can be housed in a word study notebook that each group member uses to record vocabulary and word study activities.

Vocabulary Preview: After students master the first 100 sight words, introducing vocabulary becomes an important strategy before a new text is read. The teacher should preselect words and write them on note cards. The teacher then presents the words to students and assists them in defining the words. During the reading, the vocabulary words are again discussed as they relate to their meaning in the text. After reading, the vocabulary is again reviewed and often used as a way to summarize the story. It is also important to revisit the vocabulary in a systematic manner by periodically reviewing the words and their meanings.

Summarize With Vocabulary: This activity addresses both vocabulary and comprehension. After reading the text, students are asked to use each word in a sentence that tells something that happened in the story. Additionally, students can write a story summary outside of group using the focus story vocabulary.

Comprehension (New Read)

Simply stated, comprehension is the ability to understand text. The goal of reading is to understand the text, not just to read the words. In other words, skillful readers must be able to think critically as they navigate the text. As previously discussed, comprehension becomes the focus of reading instruction as students become confident decoders of text. The strategies and activities that support comprehension differ as students progress in their reading development. Most students require explicit and systematic instruction in comprehension as they progress through meaningful text. The National Reading Panel report (NICHD, 2000) outlines specific strategies that are critical to the comprehension process including student and teacher questioning, summarizing, using graphic organizers, monitoring comprehension, and examining the text structure. These strategies and the activities that support them will be presented in the lesson plan models.

There is a real need for students to be engaged in "real" reading while applying their knowledge in reading situations. Real reading can be said to take place when the parts are put together in a smooth, orchestrated performance. The most useful form of practice is reading meaningful text for the purpose of understanding the messages it contains.

Teaching reading comprehension is a complex process. Teachers must have a foundational knowledge of the content presented in the text, as well as the knowledge of the specific strategies that are most effective based on the students' developmental reading stage, the type of content, and how best to teach and model the strategy use. Each lesson plan model includes differentiated comprehension strategies as students develop their comprehension tool box.

Strategies and Activities That Support Comprehension in the Small-Group Model

The activities that support increased comprehension focus on routines conducted before, during, and after reading the text. It is important that each of these activities be completed in a systematic and explicit manner. Activities include both oral discussions in the small-group setting and written responses completed by students outside of group. See the accompanying CD 🔘 for auxiliary instructional materials that correspond to these activities.

Predicting: Predicting is only powerful when students' predictions are confirmed or modified as the text is read. This strategy assists students as they monitor their own comprehension of the text. In my experience, predicting before reading often turns into wild guessing that has nothing to do with understanding the text. Teachers must be skillful in leading students to naturally confirm or change their predictions as the text is read.

Making Connections: In this activity, the teacher helps students make important connections to the text. These connections include connections that students make with personal experiences, other texts that they have read, or other experiences that they have had in real-world situations.

Previewing Text Structure: With nonfiction text, it is important for students to examine the text structure prior to reading the text. The text structure might include the table of contents, picture captions, graphs, an index, or a glossary. Examining these features will better prepare students to navigate this type of text.

Picture Walk: This activity is especially important in the first three stages of reading instruction. Before reading the text, the teacher conducts a picture walk through the text to establish the story line, introduce unfamiliar vocabulary, and use picture clues to understand the text's message.

Building Background Knowledge: When students lack the background knowledge necessary to understand the text, the teacher must provide that information to them. Without sufficient background knowledge, students will be unable to understand the meaning of the text. Prior to reading the text, the teacher questions students to determine their knowledge about the subject and then provides them with the information they need to understand the text.

Summarizing: Summarizing is essential to a student's basic understanding of text. Summarizing includes activities such as retelling, sequencing the story or events, identifying main ideas and details, identifying story elements, recognizing cause-and-effect relationships, and comparing and contrasting. See CD 💿 for auxiliary materials including reproducibles that support summarizing.

Questioning: There are two types of questioning that are important to understanding the text: teacher questioning and student questioning. First, teacher questioning requires the careful use of literal, inferential, and application questions. Literal questions can be answered directly from the text. Inferential questions require students to make connections in the text and "read between the lines." Application questions require students to apply information to another situation. Second, student questioning encourages students to question the text as it is read. These questions are often categorized as "I wonder...." questions. This kind of questioning allows students to interact with the text in a meaningful way.

Using Graphic Organizers: Graphic organizers give students a vehicle for demonstrating their comprehension of the text. As readers become more advanced, they should be able to choose or create appropriate organizers to illustrate their thinking.

The accompanying CD 💿 provides additional comprehension materials that can be used both in group or as independent follow-up, including the following:

- Cause and Effect: Students identify cause-and-effect relationships in text.
- Circle Story: Students sequence events from the text.
- Compare/Contrast: Students compare and contrast two things.

- First, Then, Next, Finally: Students summarize through writing.
- Main Ideas/Details: Students isolate main ideas and details from text.
- Story Map: Students identify important story elements.
- Summarize With Vocabulary: Using the story vocabulary, students summarize the text.
- The Top Five Things About…: Students identify main ideas, especially in nonfiction text.

Selecting Leveled Books for Small-Group Differentiated Reading Instruction

The more time spent reading books at an appropriate instructional level, the more students achieve (Fountas & Pinnell, 2003). Leveled books serve as the centerpiece for the Small-Group Differentiated Reading Model, and publishing companies have become increasingly aware of their importance. Each reading lesson begins with rereading a previously read text and ends with the introduction and reading of a new book. Before reading, students are encouraged to predict the story line by looking at the book's illustrations. Then, with the teacher's assistance, the students modify their original predictions while they read the story. The routine of introducing a new book each day provides students with the opportunity to read five new books every week. The new book should be slightly more difficult than previous reads. Using carefully leveled books allows children to progress at their instructional level—challenged but not overwhelmed. Appropriately pacing children through increasingly difficult reading material is one key to effective instruction. However, the process of purchasing or organizing a leveled book collection to support the reading model can be a formidable task.

There are a variety of models for leveling books, including Reading Recovery, Developmental Reading Assessments (DRA), Fountas and Pinnell, and others by individual textbook companies. Selecting quality, accurately leveled books is critical to the differentiated reading process. Each individual school should decide on a leveling system that is expansive and appropriate. Once the decision is made, all books should be merged using the same leveling system. Books should be previewed to make sure that the levels seem appropriate for beginning readers. There should be some balance between more natural language books and controlled vocabulary books. Natural language books use language familiar to children to tell a complete story. Controlled vocabulary books use sets of words chosen according to the frequency they appear in language and books and words that demonstrate sound relationships in phonics instruction. These controlled vocabulary stories must rely heavily on picture support for meaning.

Selecting beginning books for children is a balancing act between natural language and controlled vocabulary books. Children have an easier time understanding stories written in familiar (natural) language but may have difficulty decoding some of the challenging words. Using controlled vocabulary in stories can be boring and unengaging for students. The answer for the most effective reading instruction is to provide a balance between these two book types.

Therefore, choosing books from a variety of sources is encouraged, as long as books are eventually leveled using the same system. A book need not be permanently slotted as a level 7 or level 8. After using the book with children, teacher teams should review books that might seem inappropriately leveled. Leveling books is a somewhat subjective activity, and there are no clearly wrong or right decisions in assigning levels.

The following criteria provide a basic framework for examining and leveling books:

- Overall length of the book
- Number of words on a page
- Number of lines on a page
- Correspondence of illustrations to print
- Legibility of type
- Size of print
- Spacing between words and between lines
- Phonic complexity
- Range of punctuation
- Range of illustrations
- Familiarity of content
- Familiarity of theme
- Complexity of story line
- Type of text: narrative or expository
- Repetitive language
- Sentence structure
- Vocabulary

Table 6 is presented as a guide for selecting leveled books to support the five stages of the Small-Group Differentiated Reading Model. A range of appropriate book levels is suggested. Many textbook companies level books using the three most popular systems—Reading Recovery, DRA, Fountas and Pinnell, which are reflected in Table 6. In the past, teachers have labored over leveling book collections, but as this process becomes easier, it is critical that teachers be familiar with their leveled books so that they are aware of the unique supports and challenges included in each text.

Conclusion

The components outlined in the Small-Group Differentiated Reading Model provide focused instruction in basic literacy elements. The strategies and activities that support these research-based components in the lesson plan are critical. Unlike other small-group

TABLE 6
Leveled Books for Reading Groups

Stage	Reading Recovery	DRA	Fountas and Pinnell
1 Emergent Reader	1–2	1–2	A
2 Beginning Reader	3–5	3–5	B–C
3 Fledgling Reader	6–11	12–16	D–G
4 Transitional Reader	12–16	11–17	H–I
5 Independent Reader	17–23	18–38	J–P

reading models, each of the research-based components are carefully integrated with differentiated strategies that are included as important parts of the daily lesson plan. The reading and rereading of appropriately leveled texts provides the centerpiece for small-group reading instruction. Additionally, the developmental word study level is also addressed with appropriate strategies and activities. The components in the Small-Group Differentiated Reading Model work congruently to provide a solid foundation for continued literacy growth.

CHAPTER 3

Planning for Instruction and Assessing Student Progress in the Small-Group Differentiated Reading Model

An initial and ongoing system of assessment is critical to teaching beginning reading. Prior to beginning small-group differentiated reading instruction, it is essential to assess the literacy knowledge of each student. The ERSI, developed by Morris (1998), provides reliable and essential information about students' print-related knowledge. This assessment is useful for students in kindergarten and the beginning of first grade. The teacher uses this information as a guide for forming groups and tracking progress in small-group instruction. Several parts of the ERSI can be readministered to determine gains. This is particularly useful for emergent and beginning readers. As students progress through the subsequent reading stages, additional assessments are administered to provide ongoing information regarding fluency, instructional reading levels, word study levels, and sight word knowledge.

Three other assessments are used to support teachers with initial and ongoing placements for students as well as to monitor student progress. The Reading Review assesses students' instructional reading levels as well as fluency levels as they progress through the five stages of beginning reading. This ongoing assessment provides valuable information to teachers as they group and regroup students to best meet students' instructional needs. Additionally, word study assessments are routinely administered both initially and then as students complete important milestones in the word study sequence. These word study assessments are useful to determine students' entry levels in word study as well as to monitor their progress in this important area. The Sight Word Assessment assesses students' individual knowledge of the first 100 sight words. Teachers make instructional decisions about grouping students based on this assessment. The Reading Review, word study assessments, and Sight Word Assessment provide teachers will valuable information necessary for planning and delivering powerful literacy instruction. All assessment information is available on the CD .

ERSI (Early Reading Screening Instrument)

Several research studies verify the effectiveness of the ERSI. In a study conducted by Lombardino, Defillipo, Sarisky, and Montgomery (1992), the predictive validity of the ERSI was verified. The researchers found that the ERSI, when given to kindergarten students near the end of the year, correlated 0.73 with the Woodcock-Johnson Comprehension Subtest administered to the same students at the end of first grade. Other studies in North Carolina reached similar conclusions. For example, in a rural county, student performance on the ERSI at the beginning of first grade correlated 0.70 with their passage-reading ability at the end of first grade (Perney, Morris, & Carter, 1997).

The ERSI is administered on an individual basis and takes about 20 minutes to complete and evaluate the results. This assessment looks at the basic skills that researchers (e.g., Chall, 1987; Dowhower, 1987; Reitsma, 1988) believe are critical to early reading success. These areas include the following:

- Alphabet recognition and production: Does the student recognize both upper- and lowercase letters? Can the student reproduce letters in random order?

- Concept of word: Can the student track print? Does he or she understand what a word is and that words make up the English language?

- Sight words: Does the student recognize some basic sight words in isolation?

- Phoneme awareness: Does the student hear individual sounds in words? How does this relate to his or her development in spelling?

- Decodable words: Can the student decode simple unknown words using phonics knowledge?

Although the ERSI is effective in determining students' knowledge of printed words, perhaps the most important assessment as it relates to the ongoing reading process is the Reading Review, which accurately determines instructional reading and fluency levels for students. The Reading Review is a brief assessment used as a student reads 100 words in a new book. As the child reads, the teacher simply records errors made by the student. The teacher then uses this information to determine if the level is too easy, too difficult, or at the correct instructional level. Fluency rates are strong indicators for student progress toward independence. The Reading Review is appropriate to use beginning with the Fledgling Reader stage.

Administration of the ERSI

This section gives step-by-step directions on how to administer the ERSI. See CD for assessment materials including the individual student test and abbreviated teacher directions.

1.1 Alphabet

Section 1.1 of the test evaluates the student's knowledge of the alphabet and production of letters. Many students come to school able to identify and reproduce many of the letters of the alphabet, but others may lack these skills and require further instruction. Not every student needs to review every letter. Assessment will reveal to the teacher who needs extensive help learning the alphabet.

Alphabet Recognition

In this portion of the assessment, students are asked to both identify and produce the letters of the alphabet.

Procedure: Using a random list of upper- and lowercase letters such as the one below, ask the student to name the letters as you point to them:

A F K P W Z	a f k p w z
B H O J U	b h o j u
C Y L Q M	c y l q m
D N S X L	d n s x l
E G R V T	e g r v t

Scoring: Using the ERSI Individual Score Sheet, Section 1.1, record the information noting errors and no-attempts for each letter. If the student is unable to recognize the letter, simply circle the letter to note nonrecognition. If the student gives the incorrect letter response, write the incorrect letter above the letter. It is important to note that reversals are counted as errors, but self-corrects are counted as correct and are indicated with a check (✓) beside the first incorrect response. Record the number of correctly identified upper- (0–26) and lowercase (0–26) letters.

Alphabet Production

This task is more advanced than alphabet recognition. The student will complete this section of the test on the lined form.

Procedure: Begin by telling the student to write either an upper- or lowercase letter (not both). Using the order of the alphabet in the previous section, call out the letters in random order. If the student is unable to write a letter, record that information on Section 1.1 of the Individual Score Sheet. The following shows a student alphabet production assessment that reflects two errors.

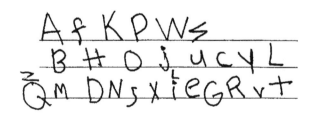

Scoring: Count each correctly produced letter. In this subtest, reversals (such as *b-d*) are counted as correct (unlike the recognition section). However, upside down reversals (such as *p*-d) are counted as incorrect.

To obtain the Alphabet subtest score, add the scores from each section together:

Recognition Upper (0–26) (a)
Recognition Lower (0–26) (b)
Reproduction (0–26) (c)

The top score, if there were no errors, would total 78. Write these scores in the scoring section at the top of the Individual Score Sheet.

Upper		Lower		Prod.		Total
(26)		(26)		(26)		(78)
(a)	+	(b)	+	(c)	=	

1.2 Concept of Word (The Katie Book)

Concept of word refers to the beginning reader's ability to match spoken words with written words when he or she reads a line of text. This important concept is often overlooked in early reading assessments. However, before a student is able to read, he or she must first be able to track print. In other words, after the teacher models finger-point reading a sentence, the student should be able to accurately finger point to each word as he or she recites the sentence. This does not mean that students are being asked to actually read the words in the sentence. The evaluator is simply trying to determine if the student recognizes that individual words make up a sentence. Until a student can repeat and point to the words in a sentence, he or she will have difficulty learning sight words or developing the strategy of using letter sounds to decode words in text (Clay, 1979; Morris, 1993).

There are two ERSI subtests that evaluate a student's concept of word (1.2 and 2.1). These two subtests are not given in sequence. Instead, Test 1.3, Word Recognition, comes between the two subtests. To make this sequence easier to follow, the two concept-of-word subtests are discussed together because they are eventually scored as one test.

The Katie Book subtest requires the student to finger-point read three different sentences and identify preselected target words within the sentences. The three pages of the book are covered and stapled together to make a book.

Procedure: Begin by asking the student what he or she thinks is happening in the picture. Tell the student (while pointing to the picture) that the sentence tells us what is happening. Ask the student to watch as you read and point to each word. (Read and finger point the sentence one time.) Then, ask the student to read and finger point the sentence by himself or herself. After completing the sentence, quickly point to the first target word (on the first page, the word is *walking*) and ask, "Can you read this word?" Move to the second target word *rain* and repeat the question. Use this same procedure on pages 2 and 3 of the Katie Book.

Scoring: The student receives two scores—one for reading and finger pointing and another for reading the underlined words. The score sheet should be filled in as each sentence is completed. Finger pointing is scored as either correct (✓) or incorrect (**0**). If the student correctly finger points each word in the sentence, she or he receives 1 point (✓). If there is even one mistake in pointing or calling a word incorrectly, the student receives no points (**0**). Figure 3 represents the score box for the Katie Book. The student scored 2 points for pointing and 3 points for identifying words.

FIGURE 3
Katie Book Score Sheet

1.2 Concept of Word (Katie Book)

	Point	Words

		Point		Words	
1. Katie is <u>walking</u>¹ in the <u>rain</u>².	✓	₁ **0**	₂	✓	
2. <u>She</u>¹ sees a <u>big</u>² dog.	✓	₁ ✓	₂	✓	
3. The <u>dog</u>² shakes <u>water</u>¹ on Katie.	**0**	₁ **0**	₂	**0**	

Scores are combined with section 2.1. When test is completed, count ✓s for pointing and words. Record in box in section 2.1.

Be consistent in your scoring procedures to get the most accurate information. There are 3 possible points for pointing and 6 possible points for words.

2.1 Concept of Word (*My Home*)

This component provides additional information as students track two lines of print as well as identify some words in isolation.

Procedure: Begin this subtest by sharing the cover of the book *My Home* by June Melser with the student. Discuss the cover and look at each picture in the book and have the student identify the animals before beginning the test.

Then, turn back to the first page and begin reading the book. Ask the student to watch as you read the first sentence (point to each word). Then, ask the student to finger-point read. Record the student's performance on the answer sheet (**0** or ✓). When you begin on page 3, ask the student to read the final three pages by himself or herself. (There should be no more assistance or modeling.) If the student cannot continue, model and finger point the sentences. (No points should be given, though.) Word identification occurs only on the first two pages. Figure 4 shows one student's assessment using *My Home*. The student scored 4 points for correctly finger pointing and 2 points for correct word identification.

FIGURE 4
My Home Score Sheet

2.1 Concept of Word (*My Home*)

Page			Point	Word
(2)	"My home is <u>here</u>," said the bird.		✓	✓
(3)	"My home <u>is</u> here," said the frog.		✓	0
(4)	"My home is here," said the pig.		✓	
(5)	"My home is here," said the dog.		0	
(7)	"My home is here," said the rabbit.		✓	

Note: Count ✓s for pointing and words from sections 1.2 and 2.1 and record totals below.
CORRECT (point) __6__/8
Katie Book   (d)
and *My Home*
#CORRECT (word) __5__/8
Katie Book   (e)
and *My Home*

Reprinted from Morris, D. (1998). Assessing printed word knowledge in beginning readers: The Early Reading Screening Instrument (ERSI). *Illinois Reading Council Journal, 26*(2), 30–40. Reprinted with permission.

Scoring: This score will be combined with the score on the Katie Book for a total score. Transfer the combined scores for pointing in the Katie Book and *My Home* to the point box (d). Do the same for both books in the word box (e). There are 16 total possible points.

Concept of Word		
Point	Word	Total
(8)	(8)	(16)
_____	_____	_____
(d)	(e)	

2.2 Phoneme Awareness (Spelling)

It might seem to some educators that spelling is an inappropriate way to assess early reading ability. There are, however, research-based reasons for doing so. First, a student's spelling and reading ability are highly correlated in the early primary grades (K–2). Morris and Perney (1984) report a 0.82 correlation between first graders' January spelling ability and their May, end-of-year, word-recognition ability. Second, and more important, spelling gives us insight into a student's ability to read words by looking at how he or she spells words. This is because an abstract, developing word knowledge underlies the ability to both read and spell (Gill, 1992; Henderson, 1990). This subtest will help determine exactly where a student should begin in a program of word study.

Procedure: This assessment is a 12-word spelling task in which students write the sounds they hear in words. This subtest begins with the examiner modeling a "sound-it-out" spelling of two sample words, *mat* and *lip*. Tell the student that you are going to write the word *mat*. Ask the student which letter you should write down first. (Praise a correct response. If an incorrect response or no response is given, still write the *m* on the paper and say that the first letter is *m*.) Ask the student which letter you should write down next. Complete the first word. Continue on to the next sample word, *lip*.

After demonstrating the two examples, give the student the pencil and designated answer sheet. Tell the student that he or she is going to write some words. Read the words on the list (you may use the word in a sentence, if necessary). Prompts may be used only on the first and second words (e.g., What sound do you hear next?). No prompts should be given on the remaining words. Remind the student to write every sound that he or she hears in the word. The purpose of this exercise is not to frustrate children but to get diagnostic information. If the student fails to give at least the initial sound of both the sample words and each of the first two test words, stop the test.

Scoring: Scoring involves counting the number of phonemes (sounds) in each word the student writes. Six words in the test contain three phonemes (*back*, *feet*, *mail*, *side*, *chin*, and *road*), and the other six words have four phonemes (*step*, *junk*, *picking*, *dress*, *peeked*, and *lamp*). The following shows one student's responses to the phoneme awareness (spelling) subtest along with the points given for each response.

1. Bak — 3
2. fet — 3
3. sp — 2
4. Jk — 2
5. Peckn — 4
6. Ml — 2
7. Sid — 3
8. Jn — 2
9. Jes — 3
10. Pet — 3
11. Lap — 3
12. Wod — 3

A scoring guide will help you determine the number of points to credit to each word.

1.3 Word Recognition (Basal Words)

Word recognition is central in learning to read. Beginning first-grade students should be able to recognize at least a few common sight words. Students who have some basic sight word knowledge have an advantage over students who do not recognize any words.

There are two parts in the word recognition test. This first assessment is a common list of sight words, and the assessment that follows in the next section contains a set of decodable words.

Procedure: Begin by telling the student that he or she will be reading a list of words. Reassure the student that you do not expect him or her to know all the words.

is, come, good, here, like, and, other, make, work, day

Point to the words, one word at a time, and ask the student to read them. Record any attempts, especially if he or she is sounding out the word. A student who calls *like, lake* is much more advanced than a student who calls *like, tree*.

Scoring: Simply count the number of words correctly identified by the student and enter the number in the score box.

2.3 Word Recognition (Decodable Words)

In this portion of the assessment, students will need to use their ability to blend sounds to make words.

Procedure: Follow the same procedure for this list of words as was done with the basal words. The words in this list follow a consonant-vowel-consonant pattern that gives students the ability to use phonics or sound-it-out strategies. Again, record any attempts the student makes.

cap, net, win, bug, fat, mop, led, dig, job, mud

Scoring: Score each subtest (1.3 and 2.3) separately. There are 10 points possible for each test. The student gets 1 point for each word that is pronounced correctly. Although an attempt does not count as a correct score, the recorded information does provide important diagnostic information.

Calculating the ERSI Score

Use the following formulas to calculate the total score. The formula converts the subtest scores to 40 total points. Transfer the scores to the formulas, calculate them, and then add the four scores together for the grand total (round to the nearest 10th; 0.05 rounds up).

Alphabet Knowledge $\dfrac{(a\ +\ b\ +\ c)}{78} \times 10$ = Total

Concept of Word $\dfrac{(d\ +\ e)}{16} \times 10$ = Total

Phoneme Awareness $\dfrac{(f)}{42} \times 10$ = Total

Word Recognition $\dfrac{(g\ +\ h)}{20} \times 10$ = Total

Alphabet Knowledge				Concept of Word			Phoneme Awareness		Word Recognition			
Upper	Lower	Prod.	Total	Point	Word	Total	Count	Total	Basal	Dec.	Total	Grand Total
26	26	26		8	8		42		10	10		
——	——	——	——	——	——	——	——	——	——	——	——	——
(a)	(b)	(c)		(d)	(e)		(f)		(g)	(h)		

Table 7 shows how an entire first-grade class's performance on the ERSI can be summarized on one page.

Alternative Uses for the ERSI

Administering portions of the ERSI can give an objective measure of a child's individual growth. Instead of administering these parts of the test individually, the assessment can be done in small groups. For example, by administering the Alphabet Recognition subtest, the teacher can find out exactly which letters still need to be taught.

The spelling assessment also is useful to readminister as a measure of growth. Figure 5 compares Paul's spelling performance at the beginning of the school year with his performance at the end of the school year.

T A B L E 7
Class Tally on the ERSI

Name	Alphabet Knowledge				Concept of Word			Phoneme Awareness		Word Recognition			Grand Total
	Upper	Lower	Prod.	Total	Point	Word	Total	Count	Total	Basal	Dec.	Total	
Jennifer	26	26	26	10.0	8	8	10.0	42	10.0	9	10	9.5	39.5
Susan	25	23	26	9.5	8	8	10.0	37	8.8	3	2	5.0	33.3
Harrison	26	25	26	9.9	8	8	10.0	35	8.3	2	3	2.5	30.7
Leslie	26	25	26	9.9	8	8	10.0	31	7.4	1	3	2.0	29.3
Paul	26	24	24	9.5	8	7	9.4	35	8.3	1	3	2.0	29.2
Gloria	26	24	24	9.5	7	6	8.1	31	7.4	1	1	1.0	26.0
Katherine	24	24	24	9.2	7	3	6.3	25	6.0	1	1	1.0	22.5
Patrick	26	22	24	9.2	7	3	6.3	21	5.0	1	1	1.0	21.5
Derrick	25	23	26	9.5	7	4	6.9	16	3.8	1	1	1.0	21.2
Jill	26	21	22	8.8	7	4	6.9	14	3.3	1	3	2.0	21.0
Nick	26	24	24	9.5	5	2	6.3	16	3.8	1	3	2.0	19.7
Beth	26	25	26	9.9	2	2	2.5	21	5.0	1	3	2.0	19.4
Dee	12	8	6	3.3	2	3	3.1	12	2.9	1	1	1.0	10.3
Clint	16	8	10	4.4	3	3	3.8	8	1.9	0	0	0.0	10.1
Mary	14	10	12	4.6	3	3	3.8	5	1.2	0	0	0.0	9.6
Debbie	12	8	6	3.3	1	1	1.3	14	3.3	0	0	0.0	7.9
Polly	8	2	3	1.6	5	2	4.4	0	0.0	0	0	0.0	6.0
Helen	10	5	6	2.7	1	1	1.3	5	1.2	0	0	0.0	5.2

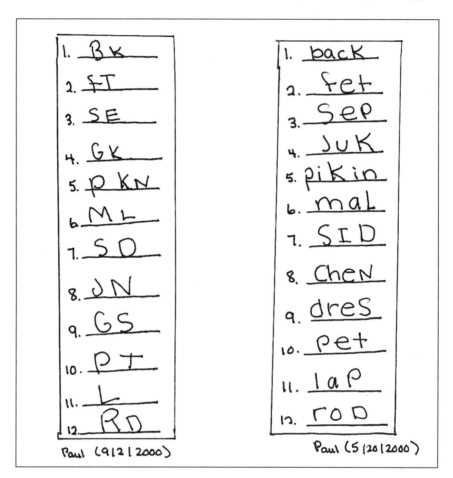

Implications for Instruction

The ERSI provides an individual profile of each student's literacy knowledge. The teacher learns which students lack foundational alphabet knowledge or concept of word. The spelling assessment is essential in determining where students should begin in word study. For example, students who know their letters and can represent most initial and final consonants are ready for word families. This assessment also identifies students who already are reading some sight words; these students can be assigned to appropriately challenging materials. Students who achieve a total score of 20 or below often need an intensive reading intervention program, along with appropriate classroom reading instruction. Table 8 provides recommendations concerning grouping based on the results of the ERSI.

T A B L E 8
Instructional Recommendations Based on ERSI Results

Name	Stage	Word Study	Small-Group Reading	Intervention Grouping
Jennifer	Stage 3 Fledgling Reader	Word families	Group A	None
Susan	Stage 3 Fledgling Reader	Word families	Group A	None
Harrison	Stage 3 Fledgling Reader	Word families	Group A	None
Leslie	Stage 3 Fledgling Reader	Word families	Group A	None
Paul	Stage 3 Fledgling Reader	Word families	Group A	None
Gloria	Stage 3 Fledgling Reader	Word families	Group A	None
Katherine	Stage 2 Beginning Reader	Beginning sounds	Group B	None
Patrick	Stage 2 Beginning Reader	Beginning sounds	Group B	None
Derrick	Stage 2 Beginning Reader	Beginning sounds	Group B	None
Jill	Stage 2 Beginning Reader	Beginning sounds	Group B	None
Nick	Stage 2 Beginning Reader	Beginning sounds	Group B	None
Beth	Stage 2 Beginning Reader	Beginning sounds	Group B	None
Dee	Stage 1 Emergent Reader	Alphabet recognition and production	Group C	Intervention Group 1
Clint	Stage 1 Emergent Reader	Alphabet recognition and production	Group C	Intervention Group 1
Mary	Stage 1 Emergent Reader	Alphabet recognition and production	Group C	Intervention Group 1
Debbie	Stage 1 Emergent Reader	Alphabet recognition and production	Group C	Intervention Group 2
Polly	Stage 1 Emergent Reader	Alphabet recognition and production	Group C	Intervention Group 2
Helen	Stage 1 Emergent Reader	Alphabet recognition and production	Group C	Intervention Group 2

Forming Initial Reading Groups

Based on the data gathered from the ERSI, preliminary groupings and instructional decisions can be made. The beginning first-grade class list shown in Table 7 on page 49 will be used for the basis of discussion. In examining the class chart, divide the class into thirds. If the class is larger, consider four groups that will meet alternately. This will allow you to keep group sizes at six or fewer. Realistically, no more than two or three reading instructional groups can be successfully taught daily.

Students in Group A possess many of the essential skills for becoming successful readers. They have alphabet knowledge, are able to track print, can represent beginning and ending sounds, and even know some words. Based on this information, these students would be ready for the Fledgling Reader stage. Additional assessment, such as the Reading Review, may be necessary to determine instructional reading level. The Reading Review will be discussed later in this chapter as an assessment to determine instructional reading level. Jennifer appears to possess word recognition skills and may already be reading simple text. Gloria has limited word recognition but appears to have all the skills necessary to begin reading simple text. Teachers need to encourage students in this stage to apply their sight word knowledge and knowledge of beginning and ending sound to read early texts. Beginning first-grade students starting in this stage usually progress with little risk of reading failure and are not usually selected for additional reading intervention.

Students in Group B recognize and produce most of the alphabet but need more work in tracking print, understanding concept of word, and identifying beginning and ending sounds. These students should begin in the Beginning Reader stage. The word study in this stage focuses on beginning consonant sounds. Because this group appears to have good alphabet knowledge and knows some sounds, it may be beneficial to assess sound recognition. This can be accomplished using the same alphabet recognition chart from the ERSI or the word study assessment for beginning sounds (Stage 2A: Initial Consonant Sounds). As you point to each letter, ask students to produce the sound the letter makes. If the group knows some common sounds, they can be omitted from the word study sequence to allow the group to spend more time acquiring new sound knowledge. Students who do not possess good letter–sound knowledge at the beginning of first grade may have some risk of reading failure. I recommend additional reading intervention in addition to the instruction given in the regular literacy block to ensure success for these students.

Students in Group C are in the lower third of the class and need immediate, intensive assistance in both regular small-group and small-group reading intervention. This "extra helping" in reading is not "different" instruction, just more instruction in a smaller group setting. These students will begin in the Emergent Reader stage and focus on concept of word and alphabet recognition. They should progress quickly to the Beginning Reader stage and begin consonant–sound discrimination. It is important to recognize that students begin reading simple, patterned texts before attaining mastery of alphabet recognition. A strong instruction plan is necessary to prevent reading failure for these students.

Planning for Larger Class Sizes

Realistically, many classes average 24 or more students; therefore, reading groups cannot meet daily. Be creative in how the students' needs can be best met. Lower level students should be seen more frequently. Plan your weekly schedule to include an extra reading group on days that have fewer outside activities, such as music or library.

The following schedule, for four reading groups, allows the lowest two groups (A and B) to be seen four times weekly. The two higher groups are seen three times a week. On Thursday, two special classes (music and gym) reduce the time available for three groups.

Monday	A	B	C
Tuesday	A	B	C
Wednesday	A	B	D
Thursday	A	D	
Friday	B	C	D

Another schedule for four reading groups allows two groups to meet per day, with each group meeting for approximately 30 minutes. Although this schedule allows for only minimal reading instruction, some small-group instruction is better than none.

Monday	A	B
Tuesday	C	D
Wednesday	A	B
Thursday	C	D
Friday	A	B

Look for additional assistance with reading groups. Teaching assistants can be trained to conduct a reading group by following a structured lesson plan. Title I teachers, inclusion teachers, ELL teachers, student teachers, and regular volunteers also have been successful in assisting with this small-group instruction. The more often each group is seen, the more powerful the instructional impact.

Pacing

The most important factor that drives student reading achievement is appropriate instructional pacing. In other words, are students moving too quickly or too slowly within a reading group? My experience has been that as cautious, conscientious teachers we tend to err on the side of moving students too slowly. We want to make sure that they have truly mastered the material. Most students don't have time to repeat what they already know in their reading lesson; this should be left to independent practice. A good rule to follow is to do what is instructionally challenging yet achievable for the group. The Reading Review and the word study assessments, which are discussed in the next section, are easy to implement and provide assistance in determining appropriate pacing.

Assessments for Placement
and Monitoring Student Progress

Although the information gleaned from the ERSI is helpful for students in the prereading stages, alternate assessment measures are needed as students advance in their literacy levels. These assessments are also included for those who choose not to use the ERSI as an initial screening. The Reading Review, word study assessments, and Sight Word Assessment are discussed in the following sections along with their uses for grouping purposes as well as monitoring student progress.

The Reading Review

For schools that have a standard assessment in place for determining instructional reading levels, I recommend staying with that assessment. There is no need to reinvent the wheel. Therefore, use the information that is already provided and use the Reading Review as a tool to informally monitor student progress. Although running records are important in diagnosing particular strengths and weaknesses in readers, a complete running record may not be necessary to determine when to move a group to the next reading level. A simplified version of the traditional running record model, the Reading Review, serves this purpose as well as acting as an oral reading fluency measure. See CD ⊙ for Reading Review in the assessment materials.

Procedure for Determining Instructional Level

The instructional level is the highest level at which a student can read successfully with supervision and support by the teacher. This "zone of proximal development" is the place where students are ripe for instruction (Vygotsky, 1978). Children learn best when they receive help from experts on tasks that would be too difficult for them to accomplish on their own (Vygotsky). The Reading Review is a quick assessment that can be completed with relative ease, allowing teachers many more chances to record children's oral reading than if they were completing a more complex running record.

Begin by selecting a book that the student has never read before as a basis for the assessment, and mark a 100-word passage. (Do not include words on the cover or title page.) For early readers, a picture walk of the book is appropriate. More advanced readers should be given only the title and a brief introduction to the book. Then the student should begin reading the passage. Using the Reading Review, the teacher simply makes a check whenever the student misses a word. Words that are self-corrected by the student within three seconds are not counted as mistakes. Proper nouns (names, cities, countries, and so forth) are counted as incorrect the first time only. If the student skips a line, it is counted as one mistake. If the student does not know a word, wait three seconds and then tell him or her the word and count it as one mistake. When the initial passage is completed, quickly check to determine the percentage of correctly read words, counting one point for each mistake. If the student reads with a 98% or above accuracy rate, the book is too easy and a book at the next highest level should be tested. Students reading a passage at 93%–97% accuracy are reading a book at the appropriate instructional level. For students reading below a 93% accuracy rate, complete another Reading Review at the next lowest level until an accuracy rate of between 93% and 97% is reached. Following is the information necessary to determine appropriate instructional levels:

98%–100%	**Independent Level**	
	Move to the next level	
93%–97%	**Instructional Level**	
	Remain at present level	
Below 93%	**Frustration Level**	
	Move down a level	

This assessment also can be used for students reading at a lower level by using 50 words instead of 100. The accuracy rate is determined by counting off two points for each mistake. Be sure that the test is administered consistently among readers by following the same procedures for all students for the most reliable information. Keep in mind that Reading Reviews are not appropriate in the earliest reading stages. Students must first be confident in tracking print and have substantial sight word recognition before this assessment is valid, generally around mid–first grade for average students.

Although it may not always be possible to group students based on their exact instructional levels, the Reading Review is useful for group placement. Reading groups should remain flexible as students are routinely assessed and placed in groups that most accurately reflect appropriate instructional levels. Reading Reviews allow teachers to collect dozens of samples of a child's reading as he or she progresses through the year.

Determining Fluency Rates

A fluent reader is one whose decoding processes are automatic and accurate and who has the expression necessary to comprehend the text's message. This fluent reading requires little conscious attention to word recognition as the student comprehends text. A student's fluency rate at the Fledgling Reader stage and above is easy to obtain. (The fluency rate does not need to be determined at the Emergent or Beginning Reader stage because students in these stages are basically memorizing and finger pointing to simple text.) Using a watch with a second hand, the teacher records the number of words read correctly in one minute. Words self-corrected within three seconds are scored as accurate. Omitted words, substitutions, and hesitations of more than three seconds are counted as errors. The number of words read correctly in one minute is called *oral fluency rate.*

Determining oral fluency rates for early readers can be difficult. Fifty words per minute is often cited as an average first-grade rate (see Morris, 1999), but at what point in first grade? Based on my experience, the following benchmarks might be useful for defining appropriate fluency rates for fledgling, transitional, and independent readers.

Stage	Fluency Rate (words correct per minute)
3—Fledgling	20
4—Transitional	40
5—Independent	60

It is important to ensure that students reach some minimum fluency rates before proceeding to more challenging levels. When teachers begin working with instructional reading levels, there is often great excitement and enthusiasm as students begin to progress. Teachers must recognize the delicate balance between the three aspects of fluency: accuracy, rate, and expression (prosody). Instructional reading level should not be selected based solely on accuracy rate with no attention to rate or prosody. Students need to remain on appropriate levels of text to build fluency. I like to use the following example to help explain this process: I would never ask a new driver to drive faster if he was running off the road and hitting mailboxes. Let's learn to drive between the lines and then we can learn to drive faster.

In the same fashion, readers need accuracy before they can build fluency rate. Table 9 provides a basic guideline that can aid your professional judgment, based on the work of Hasbrouck and Tindal (2006). The table provides fluency rates at the 50 percentile as well as risk indicators. The two numbers are unique yet can provide important insight. A 50 percentile score of 23 words correct per minute (wcpm) means 49 students in first grade had higher fluency rates during the winter measure. Whereas, a benchmark risk indicator, such as a DIBELS benchmark score, indicates the level of risk for reading failure. (Free grade-level passages and benchmark scores may be downloaded from the DIBELS website: dibels.uoregon.edu.) A first-grade student reaching a score of 40 wcpm by the end

TABLE 9
Grade Level, Book Level, and Fluency Rates

Grade Level	Book Levels	Fluency Range 50 percentile	Benchmark Risk Indicators End of Year Benchmark DIBELS
Students who reach 20 wcpm can begin to work on fluency rates.			
First Grade	3–16 EIL 3–17 DRA C–I F&P	Winter 23 wcpm Spring 53 wcpm	Minimum 40 wcpm by end of first grade
Do not proceed to second-grade book levels without reaching minimum fluency rate of 40 wcpm.			
Second Grade	17–20+ EIL 18–28 DRA J–M F&P	Fall 51 wcpm Winter 72 wcpm Spring 89 wcpm	Minimum 90 wcpm by end of second grade
Do not proceed to third-grade book levels without reaching minimum fluency rate of 90 wcpm.			

Note. EIL = Early Intervention Level (Reading Recovery level); DRA = Developmental Reading Assessment; F&P = Fountas and Pinnell; wcpm = words correct per minute; DIBELS = Dynamic Indicators of Basic Early Literacy Skills of first grade would have a low risk of reading failure (he is on track for reading success). First-grade students should be reading a minimum of 40 wcpm or higher (notice that even a 50 percentile student can read 53 wcpm at the end of first grade) before proceeding to grade-level materials for second grade. Teachers also can use the Oral Reading Fluency Rating Scales (see CD ⊙ for these assessment materials) for benchmarks for the beginning, middle, and end of first, second, and third grades.

Benchmark Books

To complete the Reading Review, a set of benchmarks must be dedicated to the assessment process. Several textbook companies offer sets of these books, or each school or group of teachers can meet and decide books at each level that seem to be the most representative. These benchmark books are used for Reading Reviews for ongoing assessment as well as for assisting in making decisions about when to move individuals or the reading group to the next level. If most students in the group do well with the Reading Review at the current book level, the teacher should be confident about moving to the next level. Conversely, students who do poorly could be shifted to a lower reading group.

Recognizing Reading Levels in Literacy Instruction

The assessment of student reading levels in the Reading Review gives additional information for planning in a balanced literacy program. Although the instructional reading level is optimal for small-group instruction, there also is a place for text that is at an independent reading level or even a frustration reading level.

Reading Level	Appropriate Place in Balanced Reading Model
Independent (98%–100% accuracy)	Books to use for independent reading, take-home reading, literacy centers
Instructional (93%–97% accuracy)	Books for use in small-group differentiated reading
Frustration (Below 93%)	Books for shared reading or teacher read-aloud

Independent Level

Daily independent reading is critical to total literacy development. This gives students the opportunity to develop fluency and allows them to experience the sheer pleasure of reading a book independently. As appropriate instructional levels for reading are determined, the appropriate independent levels also are established. If a student is reading at an instructional level 8, books at level 7 or below would be appropriate for independent reading. Reading these books helps students review what they already know. Such reading requires less energy and intensity so that readers become more confident. Additionally, independent reading allows students to focus on the meaning of the text. Although independent reading is important, we also must recognize that this reading by itself will not move the reading process forward. For this to take place, the instructional level must be addressed.

Instructional Level

What happens when students are given books at their instructional level for small-group differentiated reading? With the support of the teacher, it pushes students beyond their current reading level. The difficulty of the text and tasks needs to be beyond the level at which the student is already capable of independent functioning. Reading at the instructional level also allows students to build the use of effective cueing systems: Does it look right, does it sound right, does it make sense? Additionally, students are able to use prior knowledge to solve new challenges. Using appropriate instructional levels in combination with an effective reading model enables readers to strengthen their reading processes. Although it is tempting to rely on speed and accuracy as the only indicators for instructional reading level, there are other factors that must be taken into consideration.

Frustration Level

Books that are clearly too difficult should never be used in small-group or independent reading situations. Reading books that are too difficult becomes a matter of saying one word after another in a laborious reading of isolated words. Students quickly lose the meaning of the text and become frustrated and dislike reading. These students are unable to use known strategies to become better readers. Additionally, these students may begin to withdraw or misbehave when they lose self-confidence. Many students who remain unmotivated to read have been continually trapped in their frustration reading levels.

Books that cannot be successfully read by students have an important place in balanced literacy instruction. During shared reading and read-aloud, the teacher has an opportunity to share these books with students. Stories rich in content and story structure provide opportunities for development of knowledge and reading comprehension skills. These reading experiences also provide motivation for students as they explore a variety of genres unavailable at their instructional reading level.

Word Study Assessments

Perhaps the most neglected yet important part of the reading process is word study. Most teachers are aware of the importance of instructional reading level and in many instances have these assessments in place. Word study, however, is generally taught in whole-group instruction and grounded in grade-level standards. Any word study in small-group instruction is generally a review of the whole-group skill. This might work well for grade-level students but for students who are significantly behind or students who are advanced, this routine is meaningless. As teachers become more aware of their students' word study levels, they will become more skillful in delivering both whole-group and small-group instruction.

Basically, the word study assessments provided are simple spelling tests (see CD 🔘 for assessment materials). Each assessment is geared to a particular stage in word study development. These assessments can be used prior to grouping by administering them in whole group. For example, a second-grade teacher might administer the assessment for vowel patterns 1 (common vowel patterns) at the beginning of the school year. The teacher would then review the assessments and give the next assessment (vowel patterns 2) to those who passed with 80% or better accuracy. Many teachers are consumed by district-level assessment demands. These assessments, therefore, were developed to be time efficient and provide important information to guide small-group instruction. Once an initial word study placement is made, the teacher follows a specific scope and sequence as students progress with the prescribed word study (see CD 🔘). When the group finishes the sequence, the word study assessment is given to the group. The teacher then reviews the results and makes critical word study decisions. Again, consider 80% or better accuracy as an indicator to move to the next word study stage. Suppose a group just completed the spelling assessment for vowel patterns 1. The group assessment results showed that four of the six students reached mastery; however, the other two scored 70% and 50%. The teacher, at this point, could look for common mistakes and plan for a week of reteaching. Most likely, the student scoring 70% will pass the next assessment but the other student may not reach proficiency. If this is the case, look for another group placement for that student. These basic vowel patterns cannot be overlooked and provide critical word pattern knowledge. Another option is to provide additional assistance for the student in vowel patterns outside of group time. Finally, the student could work between two groups, one that is going back through the first set of vowel patterns as well as the group that is moving to the second set of vowel patterns. This gives the student an opportunity to "catch up" in their vowel pattern knowledge.

If the ERSI was administered, those results concerning alphabet recognition and production can be used. Teachers should document each student's progress through the word study sequence and pass the information along as the student matriculates up the grades. Many times, students repeat instructional skills that they have already mastered.

Consider the lesson scope and sequences that are provided for word study as a pacing guide. Each lesson in the sequence is for one day of instruction. A rule of thumb is to never stay longer on a pattern than the sequence dictates. I have found that it is more useful for students to be exposed to all of the patterns as they begin to see relationships among words. On the other hand, if the teacher feels that a group has mastered the patterns earlier that the sequence indicates, move to the next pattern sequence. In other words, lessons can be skipped but not added.

Sight Word Assessment

The mastery of the first 100 sight words is an important milestone in the beginning reading process. It is one of the critical pieces in determining when to adjust early instructional reading levels. The Sight Word Assessment (see CD 🔘) can be given initially to make sound instructional decisions and then for monitoring purposes as students master the first 100 sight words.

Tracking Student Progress

It is essential for teachers to track student growth. In many instances, students, especially struggling readers, are given instruction that is either too easy or too difficult. In addition, typically too much time is spent in the beginning of the year assessing students' literacy levels. A Student Reading Assessment Profile (see CD 🔘 for assessment materials) can be kept in the permanent record of each student to help keep a record of assessment data that is critical as teachers plan for instruction and as students matriculate to the next grade level. Another tracking tool that is important for teachers is the Classroom Assessment Profile (see CD 🔘). This document allows the teacher to view the literacy levels of all the students in the classroom to make grouping decisions.

Conclusion

The first step in teaching a student to read is to determine what he or she can do as a reader. Although beginning readers are generally viewed as a homogeneous group, there are important prerequisites to reading that should be considered individually. The ERSI assesses alphabet knowledge, concept of word, sight word vocabulary, phoneme awareness (spelling), and the ability to decode simple phonemically correct words. The initial assessment data provided by the ERSI serves three major functions. First, it assists teachers in placing students in appropriate instructional groups based on individual strengths and weaknesses. Second, the ERSI provides initial assessment data that can be used as a benchmark against which a student's future progress can be compared. Third, the ERSI can be used for early identification of at-risk readers.

Although the ERSI provides important initial instructional data, it is only a start. Assessment, to be effective, must be an ongoing process. The Reading Review, word study, and sight word assessments should be included as integral parts of this reading model as they guide critical instructional decisions. These assessments provide important pacing information that is critical for maximum reading growth. As the stages of reading unfold in the following chapters, the need for ongoing assessments and the role they play in both monitoring student progress and making instructional decisions will become clear.

CHAPTER 4

Stage 1: Emergent Reader

Characteristics of Emergent Readers

Emergent readers are beginning to exhibit some characteristics of early readers. They are typically beginning to midyear kindergartners who recognize less than half the alphabet. In some cases, they may know none of the alphabet letters. It is important to determine the letters each student knows for grouping purposes. Another characteristic of emergent readers is their inability to track print or point to each word as they read. Emergent readers know few if any sight words. Finally, emergent readers generally lack phonemic awareness; they are unable to attend to individual sounds within spoken words. Emergent readers have special needs in the area of written language learning that are difficult to meet in the context of whole-class instruction. It is, therefore, important to address all of the critical needs of emergent readers in a small-group setting.

Texts for Emergent Readers

Exposing emergent readers to text at this early stage supports their reading efforts and affirms them in the belief that they will become readers. Enlarged text is helpful for emergent readers. This text can be in the form of a Big Book, poem, song, or student-generated story. The structure must be simple so that pictures tell the story. For emergent readers, one or two sentences per page are appropriate. It is important that the text be repetitive, with only one or two word changes on each page. Rhyming within the text also is helpful in supporting emergent readers. Poems and familiar chants are excellent resources for these students because the familiarity makes the task of tracking print easier. Also, nursery rhymes (for example, "Peas Porridge") often contain a number of high-frequency words (e.g., *hot, cold, in, the, days, old*):

> Peas Porridge
> Peas porridge hot,
> Peas porridge cold,
> Peas porridge in the pot,
> Nine days old.

Student-generated stories, in which each group member contributes a sentence, also may serve as appropriate texts. Students can dictate an original story, or the teacher can provide a structure and let the children fill in the blanks.

I like to play tag.
I like to play ball.
I like to play soccer.
I like to play tennis.
I like to play games.
I like to play _____.

Whatever the text, it will be the new read used for emergent readers the first day and the reread for the next day. Rotating Big Books, poems, songs, and student-generated stories provides variety and keeps the students' attention. Once most of the readers in the group begin to track print, leveled text should be incorporated. In consideration of those who choose to use individual leveled texts, the following are book levels appropriate for emergent readers:

Leveling System	Book Levels
Reading Recovery	1–2
DRA	1–2
Fountas and Pinnell	A

The first book level generally has only one line of repetitive text with one word change accompanied by strong picture support. The second level has two lines of repetitive text usually requiring students to track print with a return sweep to the next line. These two beginning book levels are extremely critical to the success of the emergent reader. Wordless books are not appropriate for these early readers. Books must provide clear, repetitive print so that students learn how to track print as well as develop concept of word. When some of the students are beginning to track simple sentences, individual books should take the place of enlarged text.

Instructional Strategies and Activities in the Emergent Reader Lesson Plan

Fluency (Rereading)

Beginning fluency development includes learning to track print and developing concept of word. Begin the lesson by rereading yesterday's new read. Initially, the teacher provides full support during the rereading using a strategy called echo reading. The teacher reads the first page, and then the students read the same page together as the teacher points to each word on an enlarged text; if individual books are used, students point to their own text. The second page of the story is read in the same way. After several pages of echo reading, the students are encouraged to read chorally using picture support with little teacher assistance. Echo reading on the first several pages is important to get students "into the story," providing them with character names and repetitive sentence patterns used in the book. Although this is a reread from the day before, this technique is still useful for a successful reread of the story. Usually, the hardest part of the story for emergent readers is the first few pages. Therefore, providing this upfront support makes good sense.

FIGURE 6
Reading Lesson Plan: Emergent Reader (Stage 1)

Group:_____ Date:_____

Fluency (Rereading) Level	Comments/Out-of-Group Activities
❏ Tracking Print ❏ Concept of Word	
❏ Whisper Read ❏ Lead Read ❏ Choral Read	
Word Study (Alphabet Recognition and Production)	
Alphabet Focus: _____	
❏ Match Game	
❏ Memory or ❏ Alphabet Production	
❏ Writing (Cut-Up Sentence) _____	
_____	
_____	
❏ Group Sentence or ❏ Individual Sentence	
Vocabulary (Word Bank)	
❏ Sight Words: 0–15	
❏ Word Wizard	
Comprehension (New Read) Level	
Before Reading	
❏ Picture Walk	
During Reading	
❏ Echo Read ❏ Choral Read	
After Reading	
❏ Recalling to Summarize ❏ Concept of Word	

Whisper reading where all students read the entire text is also a good option for rereading. Finally, lead reading where one student reads aloud while the others whisper read adds variety as these emergent readers begin to refine their beginning reading skills.

- Read a page, and then have different student groups echo read together. (For example, ask girls to read a page and boys to read the next page.) When a group of students reads a passage together, it is referred to as choral reading.
- Finger point to each word as students read, or have students finger point in their individual books.
- After completing a page, point to a word and let students track up to the word to identify it. Suppose the sentence is *The fish is in the lake.* After reading the sentence together (chorally), point to the word *in.* Then, ask, "What's this word?" If there is no response, ask the students to read the sentence again but this time to whisper read it in a quiet voice until they get to the unknown word. When the students reach the unknown word in their reading, they say it in a louder voice. This is referred to as "tracking up to a word" and encourages the development of concept of word.

As the students gain familiarity with the text, reduce support during the rereading.

- Have students choral read without your support (or with as little support as necessary). Try "stop and go" reading, offering support when necessary. This strategy allows the teacher to support or discontinue support as the students choral read.
- Ask individual students to finger point to the enlarged text (Big Book, rhyme, or story) for the group as they read. (Assist students if necessary, or have students read from their individual copies of leveled books.)
- Invite individual students to read pages while the rest of the group whisper reads. The student who reads aloud is called the "lead read." This allows all students to practice rereading the text while offering individual students the opportunity to lead the group.
- Rotate lead reading by individuals with choral reading.

The following group of emergent readers is rereading a Level 1 book, and the new read is a Level 2 book. The teacher feels that most of the students in the group are confidently tracking one line of print, so in this lesson she gives them a new book that requires a return sweep with two lines of repetitive text.

———————————

Teacher: Yesterday, we read the book *In Our Classroom.* What things did we read about in the classroom?

(Students recall information from yesterday's read.)

Teacher: Let's try reading this book again today. Remember to point to the words, and we can read together. Do you remember how it starts?

Laura: Yes, it starts with "The pencils go here."

Teacher: I'll read the first page to get us started. Put your pointer finger under the first word and follow along while I read the first page.

(Teacher reads the sentence while students finger point.)

Teacher: Now let's read the page together.

(Students and teacher read together as teacher monitors students tracking correctly.)

Teacher: That was great. Now let's turn the page. Take a look at the picture. What is the little girl hanging on the wall?

Alisha: A bookbag.

Teacher: Yes, it is a bookbag, but they just call it a bag.

(Teacher points to the word *bag*.)

Teacher: Put your finger under the first word. Who knows what the first word is?

Jackson: *The.*

Teacher: You're right. Now let's all read this together.

(Students and teacher choral read.)

Teacher: Let's all turn the page. What is the little girl putting on the table?

Meredith: Some pencils.

Teacher: Yes, she is showing the boy that the pencils go here. Meredith, would you be the lead read on this page? While Meredith reads aloud, we will all whisper read along with her.

(Students and teacher read together. Teacher points to the word *go* in the sentence.)

Teacher: Do you know what this word is?

(Four of the six students recognize the word.)

Teacher: Let me show you how to figure out what the word is. If we start at the beginning of the sentence and whisper read over to the word, we should be able to figure out what the word is.

(The teacher emphasizes concept of word as well as automaticity in recognizing some basic sight words. The book is completed using choral reading and lead reading strategies. Note that the teacher might decide to keep the book a third day for rereading. This would mean that a new read at the end of the lesson would be introduced every other day. This would be a good strategy, especially for students who have not mastered tracking print or if the number of leveled books available is limited.)

Teacher: When we finish our group today, I want you to reread this book with your group partner. Take turns reading the book to one another. Remember, if your partner needs help, give them some time to think first. When you finish, put the books in your group's reading box.

(This daily routine incorporates fluency practice at an appropriate reading instructional level. The group reading box is developed as students reread with their partners the books read in their reading group.)

INDEPENDENT ACTIVITY ALERT

- Have students respond to poems, songs, and student stories with supporting illustrations.
- Keep copies of the books previously read in individual or group boxes so students can reread them for fluency practice.
- Have students buddy read, which gives them choices. Each week students choose books from their book box to read to a selected buddy. The title of the book is recorded on a Buddy Reading Log (see CD ⊙ for auxiliary instructional materials) and the buddy signs it, too.
- Try tape recording the texts and let the students finger-point read along with the tapes.

Word Study (Alphabet Recognition and Production)

Alphabet Focus

Begin word study for emergent readers by reviewing alphabet assessments completed individually or on the ERSI. Based on the assessments, create a systematic plan for "attacking" the alphabet. If the students know few letters, follow the scope and sequence for emergent readers that focuses on teaching the alphabet in a five-week sequence (see CD ⊙ for word study materials including this scope and sequence). Generally, five letters should be taught each week. However, don't be concerned that whole-group instruction might introduce letters in a different sequence. The goal is to recognize and produce all of the letters. When small-group instruction reflects the objectives of whole-group instruction, differentiated instruction is compromised. Four activities are listed in the lesson plan to practice the focus letters: Match Game, Memory, alphabet production, and cut-up sentences. Complete the Match game and cut-up sentence daily. Rotate between Memory and Alphabet Production on alternating days.

The classroom vignettes within this section feature a small group that has limited alphabet knowledge and is on the fifth day of recognition and production of the focus letters *B*, *M*, *F*, *S*, and *A*.

Match Game

This initial activity includes matching the upper- and lowercase focus letters. The teacher and the students should have a set of upper- and lowercase letters for this activity. Using the letter cards provided (see CD ⊙ for word study materials including letter cards), have students match lowercase letters to uppercase letters. Be sure to have the children say the letter names as many times as possible. If you find that five letters are too challenging, reduce the number of letters to four.

Teacher:	Let's take a look at some alphabet letters that we have been working on. (Teacher places the first letter, S, on the table.) Who remembers the name of this letter?
Patrick:	That's an S.
Teacher:	Good job. (Teacher continues until there are five uppercase letters [B, M, F, S, and A] on the table.)

B M F S A

Teacher:	These are all uppercase, or capital, letters. Now let's see if we can match them with the lowercase letters. Sarah, where would this letter go? (Sarah correctly places the lowercase s under the uppercase S.)
Teacher:	Good. What is the name of this letter?
Sarah:	S.
Teacher:	Yes. We have an uppercase S and a lowercase s. Can the rest of you find your upper- and lowercase S?

(The process continues until all of the letters are matched.)

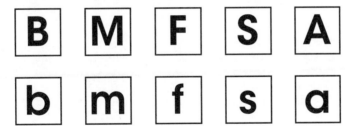

Memory

After a quick review, turn over all 10 letter cards and mix them up. Leave all of the capital letters on the top row and the lowercase letters on the bottom row. This will make the activity go faster. Ask each student to turn over one card on the top row and one card on the bottom row. If a student gets a match and can name the letter, he or she gets an extra turn. If there is no match, the next player gets a turn (see Figure 7). This game can be played on a tray and moved from player to player or with a tabletop pocket chart. Small magnets and a magnetic board also can be used. Another option is to use three sets of playing cards and monitor three pairs of students playing. This will allow students to have more opportunities to actively participate.

FIGURE 7
Students Playing Memory

Teacher: Let's review the letter cards that we have been studying. (Teacher flashes the letter cards and the students respond chorally.)

Teacher: Now I'm going to turn over these letters and mix them up so we can play a game of Memory. Ben, you can take the first turn. Remember to watch Ben so you will know where the letters are when it's your turn.

(Ben turns over the letter *F*.)

Teacher: What letter did you get?

Ben: *F*.

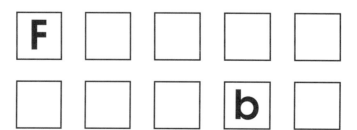

Teacher: Yes. It is a capital *F*. Now turn over another card on the bottom row to see if you can find the lowercase *f*.

(Ben turns over the letter card *b*.)

Teacher: What letter did you get?

Ben: *b*.

Teacher: Is that a match?

Ben: No.

Teacher: No, it isn't a match, so we will turn both letters back over. Remember where those two letters are so you'll know next time.

(This process continues until all matches are made.)

Alphabet Production

For emergent readers, this activity is simply the production of the alphabet letters being studied (see Figure 8). This activity can be completed in an individual student journal

FIGURE 8
Sample Spell Check

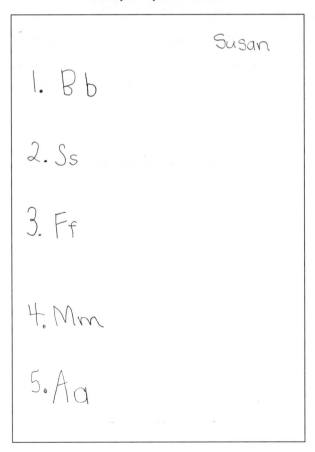

constructed with newsprint on the inside and construction paper for the cover. Additionally, individual dry-erase boards also can be and are sometimes less frustrating for beginning writers.

- Randomly call out the five focus letters, one at a time. Have students write both the upper- and lowercase letters in their journals or on the dry-erase boards. If necessary, leave the letter cards out so students can have as much support as needed. Gradually take the cards away as students become more confident in writing the letters independently.

- If students struggle with this activity, assist them by making dotted lines for the letter and letting them trace over the letters. Although this isn't a handwriting lesson, students should not practice forming the letters incorrectly. Pace the lesson as needed and remember that you may not have time to go through all the letters.

Teacher:	Let's practice writing some of these alphabet letters. (Teacher distributes dry-erase boards. The five upper- and lowercase letters are left on the table because this group is still struggling with letter formation and identification.)
Teacher:	Is everybody ready? The first letters that I want you to write are the upper- and lowercase S. If you aren't sure what an S looks like, look at the letters on the table and find the letter S. First write the big capital S, and then write the lowercase s.

(Several students immediately write the letter S, while other students search the cards.)

Teacher:	Susan, do you need a little help getting started? (Teacher reaches over and makes an S for Susan. Then, she asks Susan to make another S.)
Teacher:	Good. If you wrote the letter S (teacher holds up the letter card), an upper- and a lowercase s, give yourself a check (✓). (The teacher does not check the letters with the group until everyone has successfully written the letter S so all students experience success, even if teacher assistance is needed.)

(The activity continues as the students write the five target letters. If the activity gets too long, select fewer letters to write. As students become more confident in recognizing and writing these letters, the letter cards can be removed.)

Writing (Cut-Up Sentences)

This daily activity reinforces alphabet recognition in the context of words in a sentence. Additionally, sight words should be included to address automaticity in recognizing them in the context of a sentence. (See CD ⊙ for cut-up sentences for emergent readers, located in the word study materials.)

- Post a blank sentence strip so that it is easily visible to the group. (If you can write upside down, you can put the sentence strip on the table in front of the students.)

- Select one of the sentences provided (see CD ⊙), or create a sentence.

- Say the sentence for the group at least three times before you start writing. Have the students repeat the sentence with you. Point to your fingers in a left-to-right progression and count the number of words in the sentence. Then have students touch each finger as they repeat the sentence.

- Ask the students, "What is the first word in the sentence?" Write the word on the strip.

- As you continue writing the words, emphasize such things as starting with a capital letter, finger spacing between words, and punctuation at the end of the sentence. Because these students are working on alphabet recognition, ask the students to identify letters as you write them. Model your thinking. For example, you could state, "This is the first letter of the first word in the sentence, so I capitalize it."

- After completing the sentence, cut apart the words in a jigsaw fashion and give individual students a word or punctuation mark from the sentence. Make sure that each student has a part of the sentence. If there aren't enough pieces for all students in the group, the remaining student(s) can actually put the sentence back together.
- Then, ask, "Who has the first word in the sentence?" Continue until the sentence is complete.
- Point out sight words that are a part of the group's developing vocabulary word bank.

Teacher: Listen to our sentence for today: *The cat is black*. Listen again, *The cat is black*.

(Teacher touches a finger as each word is said.)

Teacher: Now you say the sentence with me and touch each word on your fingers.

(Students repeat sentence with teacher and touch their fingers. Repeat the sentence with the students.)

Teacher: Now I'm going to write the sentence. What was the first word in the sentence?

Laura: *The*.

Teacher: Yes, and it is in our word bank. *The* is the first word in the sentence so it must start with a capital letter.

(Teacher writes a *T*.)

Teacher: What letter is this?

Clint: That's a *T*.

Teacher: Right, and *the* has two more letters. (Teacher focuses on letter recognition.)

Teacher: Now I need to leave two finger spaces before I write the next word.

(The process continues as the sentence is completed.)

Teacher: Now I'm going to cut the sentence apart. What word am I cutting off first?

(Teacher continues cutting up the sentence.)

Teacher: Now I'm going to mix all the words up and give each of you part of the sentence.

(Teacher gives each child a word or punctuation mark.)

Teacher: Who has the first word?

Suzanne: I have the word *The*.

(Activity continues as the sentence is put back together and reread.)

Teacher: Now I'm going to put our sentence pieces in a plastic bag and write the sentence on the outside of the bag. It will be in your sentence basket so that you can practice putting the sentence back together. Tomorrow you will get your own cut-up sentence to put back together.

(On the second day of this lesson, the teacher brings out this cut-up sentence for the students to review. Then the teacher gives each student an individual cut-up sentence to put in order and glue in a journal.)

INDEPENDENT ACTIVITY ALERT

After finishing the cut-up sentence, place the sentence in a sealable plastic bag and write the sentence on the outside of the bag with a marker. Provide a pocket chart (or use the floor if necessary), and let students put the sentences together as an independent activity. Then, students can copy the sentence and draw a picture to illustrate it.

As students become proficient with the cut-up sentence activity in whole group, the individual cut-up sentences could be used as a follow-up activity.

Vocabulary (Word Bank)

Sight word recognition is the basis for the vocabulary word bank for emergent readers. Using the 100 Most Frequent Words in Books for Beginning Readers as a guide (see CD for a copy of this list located in the word study materials), begin a vocabulary word bank for the group. It is important for these readers to automatically recognize at least 15 sight words before advancing to the next book level, which includes books that no longer have patterned text. Begin with the first 5 words on the list. Use the sight word cards (located in word study materials on CD) provided or use note cards and put words in descending order (see list for word order). When the word bank contains fewer than 10 words, make two or three cards for each word so students get more practice recognizing the words. For example, make multiple cards for *is*. The word bank should never include more than 20–25 words. The group's progress can be tracked on the Watch Our Sight Words Grow form (see CD for auxiliary instructional materials). After the teacher reviews the bank of sight words with the whole group, then the group can play a game called Word Wizard (see CD).

The following group's word bank has 10 words. The teacher has two copies of each word in the bank so that the students will get more practice.

Teacher: Let's take a quick look at our word bank. I think that we have 10 words now. I'll flash the words and you say them as quickly as possible.

(Students respond chorally to words.)

Teacher: Now, let's play Word Wizard. I'm going to set my timer for one minute. When the buzzer goes off, the person who has the most words wins the game. Remember, if you get the word *zap*, you have to give me all your cards.

(As the number of words increase, the timer can be set for two minutes. The word bank for sight word recognition should never contain over 20–25 words because it requires too much instructional time from the group lesson.)

INDEPENDENT ACTIVITY ALERT

- Put word bank words in a sealable plastic bag, so students can practice reading them with a partner.
- Make copies of the sight word cards for each student to keep to review or to take home.
- Let groups of students play Word Wizard. (They love to set the timer!)
- Post a list of the word bank words. Color-code each group's words.
- Have students complete word hunts. Students look for the focus sight words in old newspapers and magazines. Then have students cut the words out and glue them on a piece of paper or word work journal.
- Make two sets of the words and have students play Memory with a partner. Students take turns turning over the cards and trying to make matches.

Comprehension (New Read)

Comprehension for emergent readers begins with a thorough book introduction. Introduce a new book by completing a picture walk. I have found that providing a picture walk is an excellent way to support reading a new text. The picture walk also familiarizes the students with the story. It includes talking with students about each page of the book and discussing what the pictures tell about the story. (I do not include the last picture so that students have a chance to predict what will happen.) Students should also make predictions about the story based on the pictures; these predictions should be confirmed or revised as the story is read. The teacher also can point to a few words that might be difficult for the students to recognize and relate the new words to the pictures. These words will not necessarily be words that students will recognize in isolation, and they should not be part of the word bank.

Teachers also can assist students in making connections to the text. Read the book and allow students to echo read the pages. As students read the text, they begin to mentally fill in the story line, confirming and modifying predictions. As students become confident with repetitive text, discontinue echo reading and begin choral reading. After reading, students should be able to recall simple information from the story. In addition, the teacher should return to the text to call students' attention to individual words as they develop concept of word.

Many teachers get frustrated with emergent readers because they believe the students are simply memorizing the words, but the process of memorizing short sentences and pointing to words in a left-to-right progression is the first stage in the reading process.

The following group will be reading a new book at a higher level; therefore, the teacher is skillful in pointing out text changes that might be new or more difficult.

Before Reading

Picture Walk: The teacher introduces a new book with a thorough picture walk. As the teacher leads this preview of the book, students become familiar with the content of the text. In addition, the teacher encourages students to make text connections as well as predictions based on the illustrations.

Teacher:	The last thing we will do today is take a look at our new book. (Teacher holds up book.) The name of our new book is *The Parade*. Have you ever been to a parade or seen one on television? (Teacher helps students make text connections.)
Teacher:	What kinds of things can you see in a parade?
Meredith:	You can see big balloons, and clowns, and bands!
Teacher:	Yes! Anything else?
Robert:	I saw old cars and people dancing.
Teacher:	So you can see a lot of different things in a parade. Let's take a look at the pictures in our book and see what was in this parade.

(Teacher continues the picture walk through the book, pointing out picture clues and making text connections that will support the students in a successful read of the new book. Note that if students have a copy of the book during the picture walk, they are often distracted. You might want to "control" the picture walk with the teacher having the only copy.)

During Reading

Echo and Choral Reading: Emergent readers need significant support to read the text. Echo reading gives students the opportunity to hear the teacher read first and then repeat the reading of the page. After the first two or three pages are echo read and the repetitive story line is established, the students are encouraged to look at the picture clues and read the page chorally with the teacher.

Teacher:	Now let's go back and read *The Parade*. (Teacher distributes books to the students.) I'll read the first page and you point to the words in your book while I read. When I finish reading, you will read the page to me. You will be my echo. (Teacher reads.)
Teacher:	Now it's your turn. Put your finger under the first word and get ready to read.

(Students echo read.)

Using Picture Support: Emergent readers rely on pictures for support during reading. Although the text is repetitive, there is at least one word change on each page that is typically revealed in the illustration on the page.

Teacher:	Turn the page. Now look at the picture. What will we read about on this page?
John:	Clowns. The clowns are in the picture so we will read about them.
Teacher:	That's right, John. The pictures can help us as read the book. Everyone put your fingers under the first word, and let's read.

After Reading

Recalling to Summarize: The teacher asks students to recall all of the things they read about. Although emergent readers are primarily in the decoding phase of reading, this simple recall lays the foundation for future comprehension in more complex text.

Teacher:	Let's make a list of all the things that we can remember were in the parade. (Teacher writes as students contribute responses.)
Laura:	There were clowns and bands in the parade.
Teacher:	Good. Let me add those to our list.

Concept of Word: After reading the book, the teacher returns to the text and has students identify individual words that make up the sentences. This helps solidify students' knowledge that words are individual parts of the text.

Teacher:	I'm going to go back and point to some words in the story to see if you know them. Do you know this word? (Teacher points to the word *and*.)
(Four of the six students automatically recognize the word.)	
Teacher:	I think we have this word in our word bank.
Teacher:	Do you know this word? (Teacher points to the word *like*.)
(Students do not respond.)	
Teacher:	We can figure out this word if we whisper read up to this word. Let's try it. Do you remember how it started? *We like the clowns.* Yes, this word is *like*.
Teacher:	We will read this book again tomorrow.

Comments

The lesson plan form includes space for teacher comments. Use this section to make notes on specific problems or successes. This will allow you to make decisions regarding the pace of instruction (i.e., whether to move forward or to review). Additionally, use this space to record independent activities that the group will complete. See Figure 9 for a completed lesson plan for emergent readers.

FIGURE 9
Completed Reading Lesson Plan: Emergent Reader (Stage 1)

Group: _Sharks_   Date: _Dec. 1, 2008_

Fluency (Rereading) Level _In Our Classroom_ _1_ ☑ Tracking Print ☑ Concept of Word ☑ Whisper Read ☑ Lead Read ☑ Choral Read	Comments/Out-of-Group Activities _Reread In Our Classroom with a partner._
Word Study (Alphabet Recognition and Production) Alphabet Focus: _B, S, M, F, A_ ❑ Match Game ❑ Memory or ☑ Alphabet Production ❑ Writing (Cut-Up Sentence) _The cat is black._ ☑ Group Sentence or ❑ Individual Sentence	_Letter Hunt: B, S, M, F, A Cut and paste letters_ _Cut and paste individual sentence._
Vocabulary (Word Bank) ☑ Sight Words: 0–15 ☑ Word Wizard	
Comprehension (New Read) Level _The Parade_ _2_ **Before Reading** ☑ Picture Walk **During Reading** ☑ Echo Read ☑ Choral Read **After Reading** ☑ Recalling to Summarize ☑ Concept of Word	

When to Move to the Next Stage

When students know at least half of the alphabet, move to Stage 2: Beginning Reader. Word study placement rather than reading level will dictate the lesson plan selection. After students recognize and produce half the alphabet, students will begin sorting picture cards by beginning consonant sounds as well as completing the alphabet sequence. The Reading Review is not appropriate for emergent readers who are still learning to track print and are limited in word knowledge. Instructional reading level is another matter. As previously discussed, students who can confidently track print with a return sweep to the next line and recognize at least 15 sight words are ready to move into simple text that is not patterned, generally a Reading Recovery Level 3 book. If some students' readiness is questionable, other options are available. Provide additional individual assistance with a tutor or older student, or allow the borderline students to meet with an emergent reader group and a beginning reader group for a time period to determine if they can move ahead successfully. It is better to move on to the next stage too quickly than to remain at a level at which students are left unchallenged. If the new stage presents too much of a challenge, return to the previous stage.

Conclusion

Traditional reading instruction often discourages small-group contextual reading until students have mastered basic alphabet and phonemic awareness skills. Educators should not leave basic skills acquisition to chance; these skills should be included in carefully structured reading lessons for emergent readers. In these small instructional groups, teachers easily can assess and assist students with these skills. In addition, all students probably do not need a "letter-of-the-week" lesson in kindergarten. It is far more helpful to concentrate on letters students do *not* know. What about those 5-year-olds who already recognize the alphabet or even begin school as readers? If we are serious about increasing student achievement, these students should proceed to the next stage in their literacy development rather than review what they already know.

Emergent readers deal with unique challenges, such as recognizing and producing letters, learning to track print, and acquiring a few sight words. These are critical understandings and are not to be underestimated. As teachers, we are laying the conceptual groundwork for the beginning reading process. No matter what grade a student is in, if he or she is an emergent reader, someone must take the time to lay the foundation for literacy success.

There is one word of caution in implementing reading groups for young children: Keep the lessons short and interactive—always keeping in mind that challenging yet achievable activities are critical. The fast-paced lessons that are presented in this book should keep all students engaged.

CHAPTER 5

Stage 2: Beginning Reader

Characteristics of Beginning Readers

Beginning readers are starting to develop print-related understandings that underpin learning to read. They recognize and produce at least half of the alphabet and understand the concept of a word. After the teacher reads and finger points a sentence or two, beginning readers can replicate the process. In addition, these students are beginning to attend to initial sounds in words, though they may not yet identify all the letter names that go with the sounds. Beginning readers recognize at least 15 sight words automatically. Another characteristic of beginning readers is clearly seeing printed words as units in text with recognizable beginning letters. Finally, beginning readers use picture clues to support comprehension.

Texts for Beginning Readers

In the Beginning Reader stage, short, leveled books are the texts of choice. These leveled books are no longer patterned, but they still contain high picture support and numerous sight words that are helpful in supporting beginning readers. Look for books that have at least one or two lines of print per page. Picture books that use only one or two words for identification purposes are not appropriate. Books at this level should have little repetitive text, because beginning readers have already mastered the skill of tracking print. Keeping students in patterned text for too long hinders their growth as readers because they are simply practicing a skill that they have already mastered. The purpose of patterned text is to learn how to confidently track print. Once students master this skill and automatically recognize at least 15 sight words, students should be moved out of patterned text. Another element that can be helpful to beginning readers is rhyme. There are currently a variety of book companies that offer both fiction and nonfiction at this beginning level. Balancing these two genres will be important as readers progress to more advanced levels. The following book levels are appropriate for beginning readers:

Leveling System	Book Levels
Reading Recovery	3–5
DRA	3–5
Fountas and Pinnell	B–C

Reading Lesson Plan: Beginning Reader (Stage 2)

| Group:_____ | Date:_____ |

Fluency (Rereading) Level	Comments/Out-of-Group Activities
_____	
❑ Lead Read ❑ Choral Read ❑ Whisper Read	

Word Study
(Alphabet, Phonemic Awareness, Phonics)

Alphabet Focus: _____

Beginning Consonants

Lesson #: _____

Beginning Digraphs

Lesson #: _____

Beginning Blends

Lesson #: _____

❑ Picture Card Sorting   or   ❑ Picture–Letter Match

❑ Spell Check _____

❑ Writing (Cut-Up Sentence) _____

_____

❑ Group Sentence   or   ❑ Individual Sentence

Vocabulary (Word Bank)
❑ Sight Words: ❑ 15–35   ❑ 35–50

❑ Word Wizard

Comprehension (New Read)   Level

_____

Before Reading

❑ Picture Walk   ❑ Making Text Connections

❑ Making Predictions

During Reading

❑ Teacher Questioning

After Reading

❑ Retelling to Summarize

Instructional Strategies and Activities in the Beginning Reader Lesson Plan

Fluency (Rereading)

For beginning readers, fluency becomes more important to understanding text. These readers must now adhere to a wide range of punctuation, as well as appropriate levels of speed and accuracy in recognizing the words. Rereading, therefore, is the main strategy in developing fluency. Practice in rereading both in and out of the group should become a part of the classroom routine.

- If necessary, echo read the first page or two to get students started and then let them take over. If you continue to echo read each page, the students may fail to progress.
- Choral read by groups (girls read/boys read). Alternate choral reading and calling on individual students to be the lead reader while the other students whisper read. This activity gives teachers the opportunity to assess individual students while engaging the other readers.

The following group of beginning readers is reading a Level 4 book; therefore, they have been out of patterned text for several weeks. This book has a very simple story line and does not require a lot of time on comprehension. Beginning readers are still in the decoding stage of learning to read and aren't ready for books with complicated story lines.

Teacher:	Yesterday we read a book called *Red Puppy*. Do you remember why little red puppy was sad?
Laura:	He didn't have a home and that made him sad.
Teacher:	That's right. Who finally chose little red puppy to take home?
Harrison:	The girl in the wheelchair did.
Teacher:	Why do you think that the little girl chose the little red puppy?
Tommy:	Because they were both lonely.
Teacher:	Although we don't know for sure, I think that is a very good guess.

(Teacher distributes individual copies of book to students.)

Teacher:	Please remember to keep your books flat on the table. Let's read the title of the book together as we touch under the words.
Students:	*Red Puppy.*
Teacher:	Now let's turn to the first page. I'll read the first page to get us started and you follow along. (Teacher reads first page.) Now let's read this page together. (Choral read.)

Teacher: Turn to page 5. Girls, will you read this page together for us while the boys whisper read with you?

(Girls read aloud and boys whisper read.)

Teacher: Turn the page. Now boys, it's your turn to lead on this page. Look at the picture. Which toy in the basket will the story talk about on this page?

Eric: The teddy bears.

Teacher: How do you know?

Laura: The boys took the teddy bears out of the basket and now their mom is paying the man.

Teacher: Good. The picture can help us read the story so we need to always look at the pictures before we read. Boys, will you read this page while the girls follow along and whisper read?

(Boys read aloud and the girls whisper read.)

Teacher: Now let's turn the page and look at the picture. What did the girls take out of the basket?

Katherine: They took the rabbits.

(The book is completed with variations of choral reading, lead reading, and whisper reading. The teacher asks basic questions concerning the story to enhance comprehension.)

Teacher: You really did a great job reading that book. When we finish in group today, I want you to reread this book with your group partner. Then, put the books in your group book box.

INDEPENDENT ACTIVITY ALERT

- Provide a basket of "reading telephones" or PVC pipes in the classroom. Students use them as they reread to reduce the noise level and to stay focused.
- Create individual reading boxes for each student or for the reading group. The reading box should include all of the books that the students have reread in and out of group.
- Have students keep a weekly Buddy Reading log (see CD for auxiliary materials). On the log, students record the titles of books they have read to their reading buddies during the week. The reading buddies must sign the log to document the day that they listened to the reader. The teacher might, for example, require that each student have three entries every week in their reading log.
- Have a tape recorder available in the classroom. Ask students to record themselves reading one book per week. Then ask students to listen to themselves read (see Figure 11), and then reread the book to see if they can improve. The Record and Reflect sheet can be used to monitor this activity (see CD for auxiliary instructional materials).

FIGURE 11
Students Engaged in Listening Activity

Word Study (Alphabet, Phonemic Awareness, and Phonics)

Word study for beginning readers is multifaceted. Students work on completing alphabet recognition and production as well as phonemic awareness by sorting picture cards by beginning sound. After students complete the alphabet sequence, the alphabet matching activity should be dropped from the lesson and replaced with two of the other activities. Once students can sort confidently by sound, picture sorting should be substituted with matching the picture cards with the appropriate letter. This final step in the process, assigning a letter name to the sound, marks the point of leaving phonemic awareness and moving to phonics. This sequence is critical as beginning readers build foundational word study knowledge. The following activities support the word study focuses. (See CD ⊙ for the word study materials such as the word study scope and sequence, picture cards, and assessments noted in this section.)

Alphabet Focus

Continue the alphabet sequence from the Emergent Reader stage. You may choose to administer the Stage 1: Alphabet Production assessment to get a current status of students' alphabet knowledge so you can customize and focus the study. Begin word study with a quick match of the upper- and lowercase letters focusing on the names of the letters. If time permits, mix up the letters and flash them to the group for automatic recognition. When students complete the alphabet sequence, readminister the Stage 1: Alphabet Production assessment. Use the assessment information to focus on any letters that have not been mastered. When students attain 80% on the assessment, suspend the alphabet activity and move solely to sorting the picture cards and having students write the initial consonant sounds. Alphabet recognition can still be woven into the lesson.

Picture Card Sorting

Beginning readers can follow the word study scope and sequence, which focuses on presenting initial consonant sounds. Each lesson in the scope and sequence is the focus of the group session. Beginning consonant sounds are presented in sets of three beginning with the letters *B*, *S*, and *M*. The scope and sequence provides for review of previously learned sounds. Although some children have little difficulty with phonemic awareness (being able to distinguish sounds), others find the task difficult and need time to develop this important strategy.

- On the first day of the sort, go through all of the pictures to make sure that students can identify each picture name (don't use pictures that continually confuse the group), which will ensure that the activity is truly focused on phonemic awareness and not picture vocabulary.

- Always use the same pictures as the header cards at the top of each column so that there is a "known" picture card for reference. This establishes a strong picture support for the sort.

- Remember, the sort is by the beginning sound, not the letter name.

- Usually, sort three picture cards across and four down:

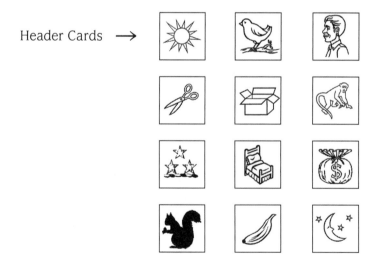

84

- Taking turns, give each child a picture card to sort in the appropriate column. Ask where each picture goes. After the card has been placed, ask the whole group to read the picture cards in the column as they listen for the correct beginning sound.

Picture–Letter Matching

As the children begin to sort the pictures by beginning sound with confidence, they are ready for the next step—sorting the picture against the letter. Thus, this activity replaces picture card sorting.

- Begin by placing the three header cards with a letter card above each picture:

Pointing to the first picture card, explain,

If we were to write the word *bird*, the first letter would be a *b*. The letter *b* stands for the first sound we hear in *bird*. The *s* stands for the first sound we hear in *sun*, and *m* is the letter that stands for the first sound we hear in *man*. Now let's sort these pictures under the correct letter cards.

- The picture card is taken away after each match to make sure the students are not relying on the pictures for clues.
- As the students become accurate and confident in manipulating the consonant sounds for *b*, *s*, and *m*, the next three consonants (*c*, *f*, *d*) will probably be easier. Follow the scope and sequence and don't remain longer on letter sets than is indicated. Based on my experience, when students progress through the sequence as recommended, they have a better concept of beginning sounds. Students will be assessed at the end of the sequence, and there will be an opportunity for review at that point.

After the sequence is completed, give students the Stage 2A: Initial Consonant Sounds assessment. Students should score 80% or above to proceed to the next stage in word study. The next step is the word study sequence that reviews initial consonant digraphs and consonant blends. After completing the sequence, use the Stage 2B: Initial Consonant Blends/Digraphs assessment. Again, students should score minimally at 80% accuracy before advancing to the next level.

Spell Check

Developmentally, beginning readers are capable of producing the beginning letter sound of words, not the entire word. During a spell check, the teacher simply calls out words that begin with one of the focus sounds and asks the student to write the correct letter that represents the sound.

The following small group is completing the last five alphabet letters and beginning to sort picture cards; therefore, Picture–Letter Match and spell check are omitted from the lesson. These two activities will be substituted after the letter sequence is complete, and students can confidently sort the picture cards by beginning sound.

———————————

Teacher: We are just about finished with our alphabet letters. Let's look at the last five.

(Teacher displays five capital letters and asks students to identify them.)

Teacher: Now let's match the lowercase letters with the capital letters.

(Students take turns matching and saying the letter names. This activity is completed quickly, so the teacher takes the letter cards and shuffles them. Then she flashes the cards to the group in random order to develop automaticity in recognizing the letters.)

Teacher: Now we are going to listen for words that begin with the same sound. All the picture names begin with the same sound as *bird*, *sun*, or *man* (point to header picture cards). We are going to put the picture cards in the correct columns. Watch, I'll do the first one. (The teacher picks up the picture card *box* and places it under *bird* and pronounces both words, emphasizing the beginning sound.)

Teacher: *Box* goes under *bird* because they begin with the same sound. Now you do the next one.

(One student has difficulty with his attempt.)

Teacher: Listen: *monkey*, *bird*. These two words do not have the same beginning sound.

(The teacher moves *monkey* into the correct column, under *man*, and pronounces both words. The students take turns sorting the picture cards by beginning consonant sounds. Each time a card is sorted in a particular column, the students read all the words in that column [starting at the top] to determine whether they begin with the same sound.)

- Ask students to find pictures in magazines or draw pictures of things that begin with the focus beginning sounds.
- Make copies of the picture cards so that each student has a set. Students can cut up the picture cards and put them in an individual folder. Several activities can be completed with the cards including sorting by initial sound.
- Have students play a game of Memory with a partner. Using the focus picture cards, students turn over picture cards with the same initial sounds and try to make matches.
- Ask students to sort and paste the cards in journals. (This activity could also be used as a form of assessment.)
- Allow students to play a game of sound Bingo (commercial games are available).

Writing (Cut-Up Sentence)

Continue to use the process for writing outlined in the Emergent Reader stage (see Chapter 4, p. 71). The teacher continues to function as a scribe for the group. Now the sentences contain some words that begin with the consonant letters being studied (see CD 🔘 for word study materials including cut-up sentences that follow the scope and sequence). High-frequency words also are included from the sight word list.

- The sentence is completed over a two-day span. On the first day, the teacher writes the sentence on a sentence strip with student input.

- When the sentence is completed, the teacher cuts apart the words in the sentence and mixes up the words. Then, the teacher gives each student a part of the sentence. The sentence is then reconstructed, as shown in Figure 12.

- On the second day, the students have individual cut-up sentences that are the same as the group sentence the day before. The students cut apart the sentence and then they put it back together and glue it in a journal.

- As a follow-up activity outside of group, have students paste the cut-up sentence in their journals. Also, students can draw a picture to accompany the sentence.

The following small group of beginning readers is focusing on the beginning consonant sounds: *B*, *S*, and *M*. Therefore, the sentence contains some words that begin with these focus sounds. Additionally, high-frequency sight words are included.

Teacher: We have read several books about bunnies, and today our sentence is about a bunny. Listen: *The little bunny is soft.* (This sentence was selected because it has several word bank words and two words that have beginning sounds that are the focus in word study.)

FIGURE 12
Students Working on Cut-Up Sentence

Teacher:	(Teacher repeats the sentence while touching her fingers in a left-to-right progression as students watch.) Listen again: *The little bunny is soft.*
Teacher:	Now hold up your left hand, and touch your fingers while we say this sentence together.
Students:	The little bunny is soft.
Teacher:	How many words do we have in our sentence today?
Students:	Five.
Teacher:	(Writing on sentence strip as students watch) What is the first word in our sentence?
Beth:	*The.*
Teacher:	Yes. *The* is the first word and it is one of our word bank words. Who remembers how to spell the word *the*?
Andy:	T-h-e.
Teacher:	What kind of letter should we use at the beginning of a sentence?
Jill:	A capital letter.

Teacher:	Yes, we always start a sentence with a capital letter. Let's leave two finger spaces before we write our next word. What word comes next?
Nick:	Little.
Teacher:	Yes, *little*. How does *little* sound at the beginning?
Jill:	/L/.
Teacher:	Yes, and that sound is represented by the letter *l*. I will write the rest of the word, and you tell me the letters. (Students name letters as teacher writes the word *little*.)

(The sentence writing is completed as the teacher guides the discussion emphasizing letter names and sounds that are currently being studied. In addition, spacing between words and punctuation is discussed. The sentence is then cut into individual words and distributed to the group. The cut-up sentence is then reconstructed and placed in a plastic bag for later use.)

INDEPENDENT ACTIVITY ALERT

- Cut-up sentence journals serve as excellent practice reading for beginning readers. Store them in the reading area, and students will have materials they can read.
- Cut up a sentence and place it in a plastic bag. Write the sentence on the outside of the bag. Put the cut-up sentences in a basket for students to put back together. Then ask students to copy the sentence and draw a picture of it. Note: When cutting up the sentences, it is helpful to cut in a zigzag fashion so that the pieces "fit" back together for the purposes of self-checking.

Vocabulary (Word Bank)

Continue to add new sight words from the 100 sight words to the words bank. When the word bank gets to 20–25 words, retire 10 or 15 of the words for independent practice. Then begin to add some new words until you build back up to 20–25 words. Remember that these words should be recognized by the students automatically and quickly.

- Review all of the words in the bank with the students as a group.
- Have students say the words as soon as they recognize them.
- Then, shuffle the cards for a game of Word Wizard (see Figure 13). In addition to the extra word *zap* that was used with emergent readers, the word *skip* should now be included. If the student gets this word, he or she must skip a turn.
- Continue to fill in the form Watch Our Sight Words Grow.

The following small group of beginning readers has completed the first 30 sight words and is now working on the next 20 words.

FIGURE 13
Group Engaged in Word Wizard Activity

Teacher: Your word bank has really been growing. You already have been through 30 words. Let's quickly flash through your word bank cards and see how quickly you can say them. Remember, many of these are new so watch carefully. (Teacher flashes cards for group responses.)

Teacher: Now let's play a game of Word Wizard. I am going to add a new card in the deck today that says *skip*. So if you get this word, you must skip a turn. I will still have the card *zap* in the deck. You don't want that card because if you get it, you must give me all your cards. I'm going to set the timer for two minutes. When the buzzer goes off, the person with the most cards wins. Ready?

(Group completes Word Wizard.)

INDEND Play Beat the Clock using the retired word bank words. All you need is a timer.

INDEPENDENT ACTIVITY ALERT

- Play Beat the Clock using the retired word bank words. All you need is a timer. Let students see how many words they can correctly identify in one minute. Each student can keep a record of his or her best time for fun. (See CD  for corresponding reproducible in the auxiliary materials.)
- Create Sight Word Bingo cards and let the group play independently. Using laminated versions of the Word Study Card Template (see CD for this auxiliary material), have students write the words in to make their own cards.
- Students can complete Word Hunts using newspapers and magazines for the focus sight words. (See CD for Word Hunt form located in the auxiliary materials.) The students can cut the words out and glue them on paper. Let the students have a contest to see who can find the most words. Anything that adds an element of competition leads to more interest by the students!

Comprehension (New Read)

The new read allows beginning readers to practice their reading strategies. The teacher carefully structures the discussion prior to reading the text to support student's reading and understanding.

- Introduce the book by conducting a picture walk using your book. Encourage students to look at the pictures while you verbalize important parts of the story. Build background knowledge if necessary, and make predictions based on the picture walk. You can also encourage students to make personal connections to the text.
- Distribute student books.
- Begin reading, and let the students join with you in choral reading as quickly as possible.
- Alternate echo reading, choral reading, and lead reading until the story is completed.

The new read for the following small group is a nonfiction book called *The Seasons*. With nonfiction text it is important to introduce all vocabulary with picture support during the picture walk. There may be words that the students are unfamiliar with or may prove difficult. Remember that the skill level for beginning readers means that they will not be able to recognize specialized vocabulary. The teacher should, however, encourage students to use picture support along with their knowledge of beginning sounds to read the text. If a group of students seems to be struggling, the teacher should wait until the next stage to introduce nonfiction text. In addition, the teacher should encourage students to make text connections and predictions as they preview and read the text.

Before Reading

Picture Walk: Beginning readers will continue to need the support of an in-depth picture walk before reading the text. These readers are now able to read text that is no longer patterned so the picture walk serves to provide them with information that's necessary for a successful reading.

Teacher:	We're going to begin a new book today that is a little different from the other books we have read so far. The book is called *The Seasons*. Look at the front cover. Do you notice anything different about the picture?
Susan:	It has real children on the cover, and they are at the beach. It looks like they are pictures from a camera.
Teacher:	You're right. This is a story about real children and real things. We call this kind of book a nonfiction book. We have four seasons each year. What season is it right now?
Jill:	It's fall.
Teacher:	Yes, it is, and another name for the fall is autumn. Let's look at the pictures in the book and see what other seasons they show us. (Teacher completes picture walk of the book pointing out pictures and words that will be important for a successful read of the story. Then, the teacher gives each student their own copy of the book.)

Making Text Connections: Before reading, the teacher encourages students to make connections to the text, which helps students in their comprehension of the text.

Teacher:	Who can name the four seasons?
Kristin:	Well, there's summer, fall, winter, and spring.
Teacher:	Good. Which season is your favorite and why?
Lindsay:	My favorite is summer because you can swim and you don't have to go to school.
Amber:	My favorite is winter because I like to play in the snow.

Making Predictions: Before and during reading, the teacher incorporates predicting as a comprehension strategy. These predictions are based on the cover and the pictures in the book.

Teacher:	Based on the cover, how do you think this nonfiction book will be different from a story book?
Laura:	For one thing, we will be reading about real things and not just a made-up story.
Gloria:	And the pictures in this book will probably be real and not just pictures drawn by someone.
Teacher:	We will see if you are right as we read the book.

During Reading

Teacher Questioning: During the reading, the teacher questions the students to increase their comprehension. These questions will help encourage students to eventually do their own intuitive questioning as they reading at more advanced levels.

Teacher: Let's read the title together. Everyone put your finger under the first word.

(Teacher and students read chorally.)

Teacher: Let's turn the page. Look at the picture. Do you remember what season this is?

Peter: Summer. The boys are playing at the beach.

Teacher: Great! Now let's read this page together.

(Teacher and students read.)

Teacher: Let's look at the next page. What clues do we have that it is still summer?

Joan: The girl has ice cream and it looks like it's melting so it's still summer.

Teacher: Good. Now, see if you can read this page together without my help.

(Students complete the reading of the book with choral reading.)

After Reading

Retelling to Summarize: After reading, the teacher asks students to summarize the text by retelling important facts and details. This can be done through discussion or by writing down the information with student input.

Teacher: Who can name the four seasons?

Joan: Summer, fall, winter, and spring.

Teacher: You're right. In which season do leaves change color?

Peter: That's easy—fall.

(Teacher encourages students to summarize now through retelling.)

See Figure 14 for a completed lesson plan for beginning readers.

When to Move to the Next Stage

Several skills should be mastered before students are ready to begin the Fledgling Reader stage. Along with complete alphabet recognition and production, students should be able to identify beginning consonant sounds in words. Students should score 80%–85% accuracy on the Stage 2A: Initial Consonant Sounds assessment. After students master initial consonant sounds, proceed to the scope and sequence for Stage 2B: Initial Consonant

FIGURE 14
Completed Reading Lesson Plan: Beginning Reader (Stage 2)

Group: _Dolphins_   Date: _Nov. 13, 2008_

Fluency (Rereading) Level	Comments/Out-of-Group Activities
Red Puppy 4	Reread _Red Puppy_ with a partner.
❑ Lead Read ❑ Choral Read ❑ Whisper Read	

Word Study
(Alphabet, Phonemic Awareness, Phonics)

Alphabet Focus: _R, D, W, V, H_

Beginning Consonants

Lesson #: _4_

Beginning Digraphs

Lesson #: _____

Beginning Blends

Lesson #: _____

☑ Picture Card Sorting   or   ❑ Picture–Letter Match

❑ Spell Check _____

☑ Writing (Cut-Up Sentence) _The little bunny is soft._

☑ Group Sentence   or   ❑ Individual Sentence

Complete individual cut-up sentence: "The little bunny is soft."

Vocabulary (Word Bank)
☑ Sight Words: ❑ 15–35   ☑ 35–50

☑ Word Wizard

Practice flashcards with partner.

Comprehension (New Read)   Level

The Seasons   4

Before Reading

❑ Picture Walk   ❑ Making Text Connections

❑ Making Predictions

During Reading

❑ Teacher Questioning

After Reading

❑ Retelling to Summarize

Blends and Digraphs. Students should master beginning blends and digraphs that are assessed in Stage 2B. Many students may still confuse several letters (e.g., *y* and *w*), but this is perfectly normal. Before moving to the next stage, students should be able to quickly identify at least 50 sight words from the sight word list. They also should be fluent and confident in finger-point reading simple texts. When making the decision to move to the next stage, look at the overall progress of the group. Remember that students will continue to review beginning and ending sounds in the context of words instead of pictures in the next phase of word study. As previously stated, it is better to move ahead too quickly than to remain in material that is not challenging to students. You may have some students who are ready to move on and some that need more work. Look for common areas of weakness and plan to reteach those skills.

Conclusion

The beginning reader is like a sitting rocket being fueled. These readers are now equipped with the basic strategies that will launch them into the world of reading. It is in this Beginning Reader stage that many slower learners and ELLs need extra time. The diligent work done with the beginning reader is well worth the effort. The next stage, Fledgling Reader, is one of great excitement for both students and teachers.

CHAPTER 6

Stage 3: Fledgling Reader

Characteristics of Fledgling Readers

For teachers who have carefully laid the foundation, the work in the previous reading stages is fully realized in the Fledgling Reader stage. Fledgling readers, although inexperienced, are equipped with the knowledge necessary to begin applying their decoding and comprehension strategies. Additionally, these students can quickly and automatically recognize approximately 50 basic sight words. Fledgling readers can easily read text with simple sentence structure and significant picture support. Major focuses for the fledgling reader are systematically studying short-vowel word families and one-syllable, short-vowel words, developing a more extensive sight vocabulary, beginning to develop fluency, and reading more complex text.

Texts for Fledgling Readers

Using carefully leveled books continues to be critical for success in early reading. For fledgling readers, choose texts that contain a variety of sentence patterns and punctuation. Both fiction and nonfiction text with moderate picture support should be considered. Books that contain high-frequency words as well as easily decodable words are also important in text selection. The following are appropriate book levels for fledgling readers:

Leveling System	Book Levels
Reading Recovery	6–11
DRA	6–10
Fountas and Pinnell	D–G

Instructional Strategies and Activities in the Fledgling Reader Lesson Plan

Fluency (Rereading)

For the fledging reader, rereading continues to be an important lesson component. Each lesson begins by rereading the book that was the new read from the previous lesson. Fledgling readers are practicing appropriate reading speed and accuracy, as well as expression. Phrasing is a central focus and is modeled by the teacher and practiced with the reread.

FIGURE 15
Reading Lesson Plan: Fledgling Reader (Stage 3)

Group:_____ Date:_____

Fluency (Rereading) Level	Comments/Out-of-Group Activities
_____ ❑ Whisper Read ❑ Lead Read ❑ Choral Read	
Word Study (Phonics) Word Families Lesson #: _____ Short-Vowels Lesson #:_____ ❑ Card Sort or ❑ Elkonin Boxes or ❑ Spelling Sort or ❑ Word Scramble ❑ Writing (Sentence Dictation) _____ _____ _____	
Vocabulary (Word Bank) Sight Words ❑ 50–75 ❑ 75–100 ❑ Word Wizard	
Comprehension (New Read) Level _____ **Before Reading** ❑ Making Predictions ❑ Making Text Connections ❑ Previewing Story Vocabulary _____ _____ **During Reading** ❑ Teacher Questioning ❑ Student Questioning **After Reading** ❑ Retelling to Summarize ❑ Using Graphic Organizer to Summarize	

- Reread yesterday's new read using varied strategies such as choral, lead reading, or whisper reading.
- The reread can also be completed by whisper reading using the "reading telephones" so everyone rereads the entire text. The teacher can "listen in" on each child as the group completes the reread.

The reread for the following small group is a fiction book called *Eggs and Dandelions*. This book is a Reading Recovery Level 10 text, which is appropriate for midyear first-grade students reading at grade level. Note that an in-depth discussion to enhance comprehension was conducted the previous day so that very little time is spent in discussion with the reread. The purposes for the reread are to practice reading simple text and to develop fluency.

Teacher:	Yesterday we read the book *Eggs and Dandelions*, and today we are going to reread the book for practice. Yesterday we found out something very interesting about dandelions. Luke, what do you remember?
Luke:	Bears like to eat dandelions, and some people like to eat them in salads.
Teacher:	I'm not sure if I would like them in my salad, but I may try that sometime. What was the problem that the bears were trying to solve?
Brian:	Mother Bear wanted Father Bear and Baby Bear to find some food. They found some eggs, but they smelled bad.
Teacher:	How did they solve the problem?
Jennifer:	They kept looking and then they found some good eggs and some dandelions.
Teacher:	OK. I think that we are ready to reread this book. We want to try to read the story today to make it sound like it was really happening. Let's read the title together.

(Teacher and students read.)

Teacher:	Turn to page 3. I'm going to read the first page to get us started. Who is doing the talking on this page?
Harrison:	Mother Bear because it says "said Mother Bear."
Teacher:	There are two question marks on this page. I know that my voice needs to go up when there is a question. I also see a comma in the last line so I need to pause there. Follow along while I read this page.

(Teacher reads with speed, accuracy, and expression.)

Teacher:	This time you read with me.

(Teacher and students read together.)

Teacher: Now let's turn to page 5. We are going to read this page together. I see some quotation marks on this page. Can you find them? What do they tell us?

Susan: They tell us that someone is talking.

Teacher: Now let's read this page together. Make sure that you can still hear my voice when you read; I will be the lead reader.

(The story is completed as the teacher models and leads students in a fluent rereading of the book.)

Teacher: When we finish group today, I want you to reread this book with your group partner. Then, put your copy of the book in your independent reading box.

INDEPENDENT ACTIVITY ALERT

- Have students reread books with a partner from their reading group.
- Assign students to read a certain number of books per week with a buddy. Using the Buddy Reading log (see CD 💿 for auxiliary instructional materials), students must record the name of the book, and the buddy must sign the log indicating that he or she listened to the student read the book.
- Use a tape recorder so that students can listen to themselves read at least once a week. Students can keep track of this activity on the Record and Reflect form (again, see CD 💿). Let students reread into the recorder, too, to try to improve fluency.
- Have students read the room. Using various pointers, allow students to read charts, poems, or Big Books read or written in whole group.

Word Study (Phonics)

Word study for the fledgling reader involves systematic study of word families and includes one-syllable, short-vowel words that no longer rhyme. The study of word families also provides a good review for beginning- and ending-consonant letter sounds in the context of words. Even if you are working with low-level readers, they should begin the *A* family as quickly as possible.

This phase of word study will be long and important. It will involve (a) sorting short-vowel words into categories (*cat* and *mat*; *wig* and *pig*), (b) committing a good number of these words to sight memory, and (c) developing competence in spelling these patterns. There are five activities that support the fledgling reader's word study: card sort, Elkonin boxes, Spelling Sort, Word Scramble, and writing. The card sort and Elkonin boxes are more appropriate at the beginning of the sequence, whereas the Spelling Sort and Word Scramble are more effective later in the sequence as students solidify their phonemic awareness. Finally, writing focuses on a dictated sentence that includes words with the focus patterns and is dictated by the teacher and written by the students. (See CD 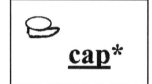 for word study materials including the lesson scope and sequence for both word families and one-syllable, short-vowel words along with their assessments and word study cards.)

Card Sort

Begin with the first three header cards for the *A* family: *cat, man,* and *cap.* These should be three words that the students recognize, or you can add a picture with the header card for more support.

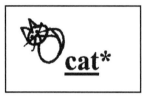 

- Demonstrate the card sort process to the students, as shown in Figure 16. For example, start with the word card *mat.* Ask the students in which column the word should be placed. Slide the card under each word and then place it under *cat.* Students shouldn't be required to say the word first and then sort it. If students know the header card and sort the word correctly, they can identify the new word by substituting the beginning sound.

FIGURE 16
Group Engaged in Card Sort Activity

- Continue to take turns, allowing the students to sort the cards in the appropriate column. After each card has been moved to a column, have the students start with the top header card and read the words in the column to determine if they are placed correctly.

- Use three cards across the top and four down. This activity will be fast paced to allow time to complete the other lesson components. Notice that a word containing a blend is included as the last word in the column. This allows students to practice the three-letter (consonant-vowel-consonant) words before adding a more complex pattern (consonant-consonant-vowel-consonant).

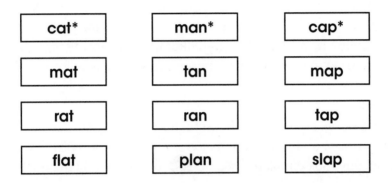

- When the group moves in the sequence to the *I* family, follow the same process. The three header cards for the *I* family are *hit*, *win*, and *big*:

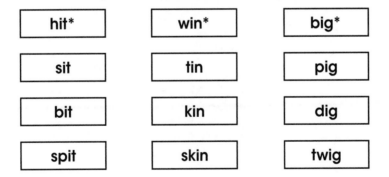

- After completing the *A* and *I* word families, the next lessons in the sequence review the two families together. This exercise ensures that students can clearly distinguish between the short *a* and short *i* sounds. Although there are a variety of combinations for *a* and *i*, remember to follow the scope and sequence using only three or four header cards across the top. For example, *man-big-cat-hit*.

- Then, move to the *O* family. Following the established routines, complete the *O* family word study.

- Review with the students by mixing the *A*, *I*, and *O* families.

- Using this same routine, complete the *U* and *E* families.

- As the rhyming word family sequence is completed, use the Stage 3A: Word Families assessment and review as needed. Look at the spelling assessment for Clint (see Figure 17). Clint scored 70% on the word family assessment, and it appears that he is still confusing the short *i* and *e* vowel sounds. Review the results of all the students in the group and customize a review based on common mistakes. Then, readminister the assessment and consider grouping options. Finally, begin the short-vowel sequence with words that no longer rhyme.

Follow the scope and sequence, and do not stay on a vowel pattern sequence any longer than is recommended. If, however, the group appears to master the patterns before the allotted time, you may skip the additional lessons and move to the next pattern. Establishing effective routines for word study is important for success in developing decoding skills. The following activity using Elkonin boxes for blending and segmenting sounds should be used in conjunction with the card sorting activity.

Elkonin Boxes

Elkonin or sound boxes are particularly useful for beginning spellers. Elkonin boxes help students as they isolate and blend sounds to read simple, one-syllable words. For this activity, use the Elkonin Box templates (see CD 💿 for word study materials), which include

FIGURE 17
Clint's Spelling Assessment

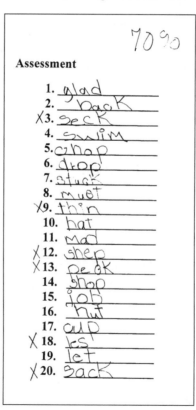

boxes for both three- and four-letter sounds. These boxes also can be constructed on card stock or purchased from a school supply store. Use three boxes for three-letter words or words with digraphs and four boxes when the words contain blends or digraphs. Laminate one template for each group member or put the templates in sheet protectors so that they can be reused.

- With the Elkonin boxes in front of each student, call out the first word such as *fat*.
- Ask the students to touch on their fingers each sound in the word *fat*.
- Using a dry-erase marker, have students write the sounds in the correct boxes.
- Finally, segment and blend the sounds of the word together with the students.

Spelling Sort

As students begin to identify patterns in words more quickly, a Spelling Sort provides students with ample opportunities to both sort and spell words. In card sorting, only one student is sorting while the others are observing. In my experience, this lack of interaction leads to boredom and off-task behavior. The Spelling Sort is an excellent way to promote more student involvement (see Figure 18) and practice and should be used in conjunction with card sorting as soon as possible. Students can use the Spelling Sort templates

FIGURE 18
Students Engaged in a Spelling Sort

for this activity (see CD 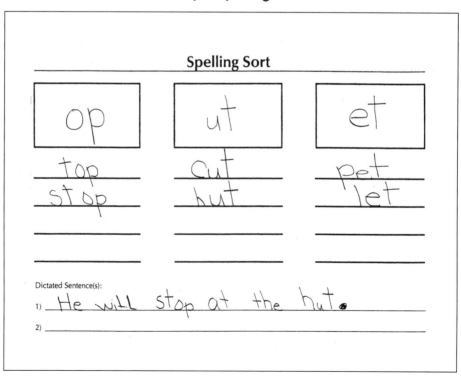 for word study materials). These templates can be laminated or put in sheet protectors so that students can reuse them. Figure 19 shows a completed spelling sort for a student in a group reviewing the one-syllable, short-vowel words for *O*, *U*, and *E*.

The following group of fledgling readers is on lesson 5 in their word study scope and sequence. The focus is short vowels that review *O*, *U*, and *E*. This group no longer uses the card sort or Elkonin boxes because they have solidified their phonemic awareness.

Teacher: Today we are going to do a Spelling Sort with *O*, *U*, and *E* word families.
              Write op, ut, et in the three boxes at the top of your Spelling Sort template.

(Teacher monitors as students write.)

Teacher: The first word is *mop*. In which family does *mop* belong?

(Students look for the pattern in the boxes and write the word under the correct pattern.)

Teacher: Yes, mop goes under the op family.

(The teacher sorts the word cards on a tabletop sorting board as a way for students to check their work. The teacher continues this process and calls out the remaining six words for students to sort.)

FIGURE 19
Sample Spelling Sort

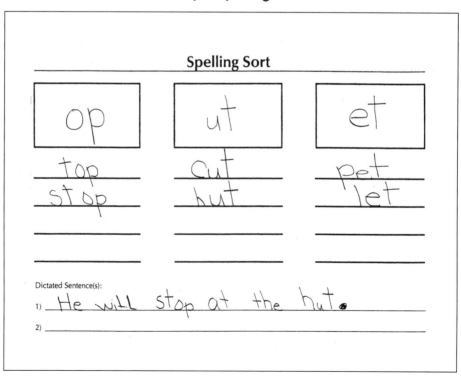

Word Scramble

Word Scramble is an activity where students physically move alphabet letters to spell words. It helps students make connections between patterns and solidify word knowledge. The word scramble activities for the fledgling reader are geared to the scope and sequence through which the reader progresses. For example, if the students are reviewing the short vowels *a* and *i*, the word scramble activity will involve students making words with these short-vowel sounds.

Make a set of letter cards for each group member (see CD 🔘). Choose seven or eight letters for each student to use. (The Word Scramble activities located on the CD 🔘 show which letters will be needed for each sort.)

The following group of fledgling readers has completed the *O*, *U*, and *E* families so next they will finish work on their word families and prepare to move to short vowels.

Teacher: Today we are going to make words that have the short-vowel sounds for *O*, *U*, and *E*. Let's review those short-vowel sounds first.

(Teacher reviews sounds with students.)

Teacher: You will need these letters to make the words.

(Teacher distributes letter cards: *o, u, e, h, t, s, b*)

Teacher: Make the word *hot*. Say *hot*. Let's touch the sounds in *hot* on our fingers. Now make the word *hot*. What letter will come first?

(Teacher observes students and assists those who are having difficulty.)

Teacher: Now add one letter to make the word *shot*. Which letter will you need to change?

Luke: You add an *s*.

Teacher: Change one letter to make the word *shut*.

(Teacher monitors and assists students.)

Teacher: Now drop one letter to make the word *hut*.

Teacher: Good job. Listen carefully. Change one letter to make the word *but*.

Teacher: Good job. Now change one letter to make the word *bet*. Which letters will you need to change?

Harrison: You change the *u* to *e*.

Teacher: Good. Now change one letter to spell *set*.

(Teacher observes as students complete the last task.)

Writing (Sentence Dictation)

This activity gives students the opportunity to apply their word study knowledge in the context of real writing. The teacher selects a short sentence that incorporates some sight words with the focus patterns. (See CD 🔘 for word study materials that include dictated sentences that correspond to each of the word study patterns.) The teacher dictates the sentence and the students write it. In the beginning of this stage, the students will not be able to write dictated sentences and will need more support.

- Tell students the sentence for the day. (For example, *The hen will hop into the truck*.) Repeat the sentence several times with the students, counting the number of words.

- Using a sentence strip, write the sentence as the students contribute. Ask who can spell the first word, what kind of letter it begins with, and what goes at the end of the sentence. Focus on the short-vowel sounds (*o, u, e*) that are a part of the word study.

- After completing the sentence, leave it posted and ask the students to write the same sentence in their journals. Tell the students to try to write the sentence by themselves, but if they need help, they can look at the sentence. Gradually, take away the sentence while the students complete the writing activity. This transitional writing activity helps students develop independence in using learned strategies and prepares them to write dictated sentences.

INDEPENDENT ACTIVITY ALERT

- Have students go on Word Hunts using books, newspapers, and magazines. Students should look for words that have the same word patterns they are currently studying.
- Ask students to play Memory with a partner.
- Using individual copies of words, have students cut, sort, and stick the words on paper or in word study journals.
- Ask students to choose two words from each pattern and write a sentence with each word.
- Choose seven or eight alphabet letters. Ask students to make and to write as many words as possible using various letter combinations.

Vocabulary (Word Bank)

Fledgling readers will be able to commit to memory the 100 sight words. Then, the word bank will include vocabulary from the text. As fledgling readers progress to more complex text selections, automaticity in word recognition and knowledge of vocabulary words will be valuable.

The following small group is working on the last 25 sight words. When they complete these words, they will move to focusing on the vocabulary in the text selections that will be important to comprehension.

Teacher: Let's play Word Wizard. First, let's all review the words together.

(Teacher flashes words to the whole group and students respond chorally.)

Teacher: Today I'm going to add a few more cards to the deck to make the game a little more interesting. We already have *zap* and *skip*. Today I am going to add *reverse* and *pass*. If you get reverse, we will go the other way and if you get pass you will pass all of your cards to the next player. Ready? I'll set the timer for two minutes and when the buzzer goes off, the one with the most cards will be the winner.

(Students complete the game.)

INDEPENDENT ACTIVITY ALERT
- Have students highlight sight words in newspapers or magazines.
- Play Word Wizard with a timer.
- Ask students to alphabetize some of the sight words.

Comprehension (New Read)

Although decoding rather than comprehension is still the primary focus for fledgling readers, there are several strategies to focus on before, during, and after reading. They include previewing story vocabulary, predicting, making text connections, questioning, and summarizing. These strategies will begin to lay the foundation for more in-depth comprehension instruction as the reader progresses to the more advanced stages of reading.

Before Reading

Making Predictions: The teacher uses predicting strategies to help students focus on the story content and to change and confirm predictions as they read.

Teacher: Today we are going to read a book called *When the Wind Blows*. Based on the title, do you think that this book will be fiction or nonfiction? (Teacher does not show the front cover.)

Beth: Well, I read a book before about the wind and it wasn't real.

Teacher: Let's look at the front cover to see if we can get some more clues.

Adam: This looks like a real story about the wind because the children are flying kites.

Making Text Connections: The teacher leads the students to make personal connections about the wind.

Teacher:	What kinds of things does the wind help us do?
Jennifer:	It can make the kite fly, and it can also help blow ships.
Harrison:	I saw some windmills, and the wind makes them blow.

Previewing Story Vocabulary: Content-related words make the nonfiction genre difficult for many fledgling readers. Providing upfront vocabulary support is an important step to the successful first read of the book.

| Teacher: | Let's look at some of the pictures and words in this book. Some of the words may be new to you. (Teacher does a short picture walk and points out the picture of the windmill, windpump, and millstone, and has these words written on note cards. She points out these words in the text and discusses the meanings of each word.) |

During Reading

Teacher and Student Questioning: During the first read of the book, the teacher primarily uses questioning strategies to enhance comprehension.

(Teacher gives each student a book.)

| Teacher: | Now let's read the title of the book together. |

(Teacher and students read the title.)

Teacher:	Look at page 3. The little girl is flying a kite and it looks like the wind is blowing. Have you ever tried to fly a kite on a day when the wind wasn't blowing? What happened?
Luke:	Yeah. I had to run and run and keep running to keep my kite up.
Teacher:	How do you think that helped keep the kite up?
Laura:	It made wind when he ran.
Teacher:	Yes, now let's read the first page together.

(Teacher and students read the first page.)

Teacher:	On the next page, we are going to read about how strong wind can help us. How is it helping in the picture?
John:	It's making the sailboat move because it doesn't have a motor.
Teacher:	Can a strong wind also hurt us? If so, how?
Ken:	Strong wind can blow down trees or blow things down like in a hurricane or tornado.

Teacher: Right. On this page we are going to read about some more ways that wind can be helpful.

(Teacher uses questioning and varied choral reading techniques to complete the book.)

After Reading

Retelling/Using Graphic Organizer: The main comprehension goal for fledgling readers is to remember and retell important information. In the following lesson the teacher uses a simple graphic organizer to retell how the wind helps and hurts us (see Figure 20). This activity will help students recall main ideas and details.

Teacher: Today we read about different ways that wind can help and hurt us. I have drawn a T-chart on my paper and I am going to write "Ways the Wind Helps Us" on one side and "Ways the Wind Hurts Us" on the other. What do you remember from the book? How does the wind help us?

Helen: One thing is that the wind can make electricity.

Teacher: Yes, and I saw on the news that we are going to try to build more windmills to help us because oil is getting so expensive. I am going to write "makes electricity" on the help side.

FIGURE 20
Sample Graphic Organizer Used After Reading

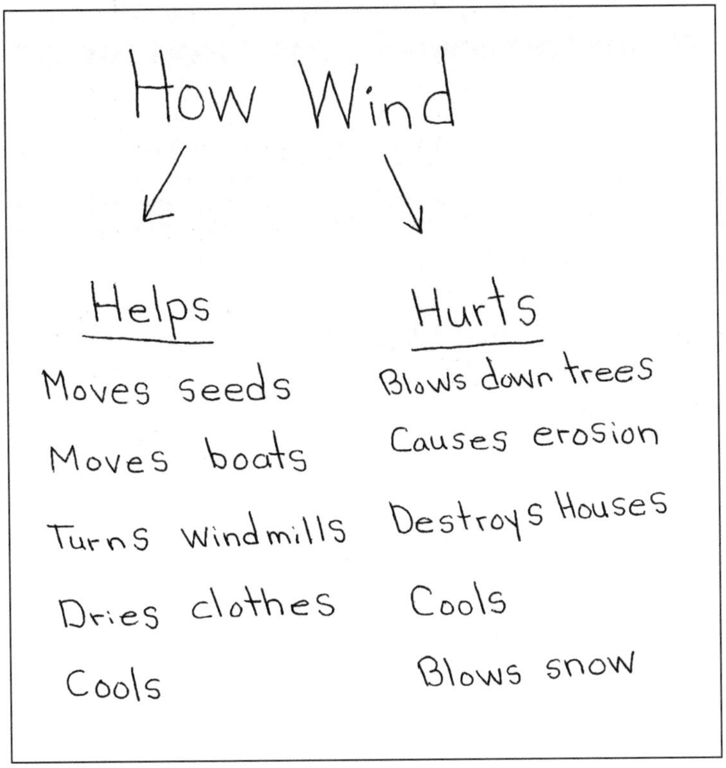

How Wind

Helps

Moves seeds
Moves boats
Turns windmills
Dries clothes
Cools

Hurts

Blows down trees
Causes erosion
Destroys Houses
Cools
Blows snow

(Teacher writes "makes electricity" on the chart.)

Teacher: Who can think of another way we read about how the wind helps us?

Deborah: It makes the sailboats move.

Teacher: Yes, let's add that to the help side. What about ways the wind can be harmful?

(Teacher completes the chart as students retell from the story information.)

INDEPENDENT ACTIVITY ALERT

When the lesson is completed, place the new read in the group or individual reading box so the students can reread it individually or with a partner. Then, have students complete any of the following activities based on the new read.
- Use the graphic organizer to write a short summary based on the story.
- Illustrate vocabulary from the story.
- Complete a story map based on the story.
- Choose one page from the story for students to practice reading with the group the next day.

See Figure 21 for a completed lesson plan for fledgling readers.

When to Move to the Next Stage

There are several milestones to consider prior to advancing to the Transitional Reader stage. Students should be able to automatically recognize many short-vowel words. Students also should be able to recognize at least 100 sight words. At this point, completion of a quick Reading Review is feasible to determine if students are reading at an appropriate instructional level (see Chapter 3 for more information). This assessment should provide ample information for determining readiness for the next reading stage. Additionally, students should have successfully passed the spelling assessment for word families (Stage 3A) and short vowels (Stage 3B). Transitional readers rely on this foundational knowledge as they navigate more complex text.

Conclusion

The Fledgling Reader stage allows students to improve and extend their existing range of skills. By combining their knowledge of prior experiences, word patterns, writing, and story structure, fledgling readers bring meaning to their reading. These students exhibit greater confidence as readers and are capable of reading and enjoying more complex stories. The next stage, Transitional Reader, advances the reader toward independence.

FIGURE 21
Completed Reading Lesson Plan: Fledgling Reader (Stage 3)

Group: **Whales** _____ Date: **Dec. 15, 2008**

Fluency (Rereading) Level	Comments/Out-of-Group Activities
Eggs and Dandelions 10	Partner read _Eggs and_
☑ Whisper Read ☑ Lead Read ☑ Choral Read	_Dandelions_
Word Study (Phonics)	
Word Families Lesson #: **39 op/ut/et**	Word Hunt
Short-Vowels Lesson #:_____	Students will look through
❑ Card Sort or ❑ Elkonin Boxes	books to find other words
or	that have same
☑ Spelling Sort or ❑ Word Scramble	patterns: op/ut/et
❑ Writing (Sentence Dictation)	
The hen will hop into the truck.	
Vocabulary (Word Bank)	Play Beat the Clock
Sight Words	with a partner.
❑ 50–75 ☑ 75–100	
☑ Word Wizard	
Comprehension (New Read) Level	
When the Wind Blows	
Before Reading	Draw a picture of each
☑ Making Predictions ☑ Making Text Connections	vocabulary word. Write a
☑ Previewing Story Vocabulary _windmill,_	sentence using the word
windpump, millstone	under each picture.
During Reading	
❑ Teacher Questioning ❑ Student Questioning	
After Reading	
❑ Retelling to Summarize	
☑ Using Graphic Organizer to Summarize	

CHAPTER 7

Stage 4: Transitional Reader

Characteristics of Transitional Readers

Although they still rely on teacher support, transitional readers are working toward reading independence. These readers have a basic sight word vocabulary of at least 100 words. Additionally, these readers can confidently read one-syllable, short-vowel words using consonant blends and digraphs. Whereas learning to read and process text has been the primary focus for emergent, beginning, and fledgling readers, there is a shift for transitional readers to orchestrate decoding and comprehension strategies. Word study moves to one-syllable vowel patterns (for example, short, long, and r-controlled). Finally, developing reading fluency plays an important role in this stage.

Texts for Transitional Readers

The leveled texts used for transitional readers should include longer stories with less emphasis on sentence patterns, which support the reader. Stories also should include some unfamiliar or specialized vocabulary, especially in nonfiction selections. These texts rely less on illustrations as clues to make meaning in context. In selecting texts for transitional readers, consider stories that allow students opportunities to practice integrating the cueing systems that answer the following questions: Does it look right? Does it sound right? Does it make sense? The following are appropriate book levels for transitional readers:

Leveling System	Book Levels
Reading Recovery	12–16
DRA	11–17
Fountas and Pinnell	H–I

Instructional Strategies and Activities in the Transitional Reader Lesson Plan

Fluency (Rereading)

Rereading continues to play an important role in developing reading fluency. Although most transitional readers can read the text accurately, they may be rather slow and choppy at doing so and may pay little attention to punctuation. Without mastery of speed, accuracy, and expression, it is difficult to comprehend the text's message. One way to address this concern is for the teacher to become a part of the rereading process by alternating turns with the students. This oral reading provides a fluent model for the students

FIGURE 22
Reading Lesson Plan: Transitional Reader (Stage 4)

	Level	Comments/Out-of-Group Activities

Group:_____ Date:_____

	Level	Comments/Out-of-Group Activities

Fluency (Rereading)   Level   Comments/Out-of-Group Activities

❑ Whisper Read   ❑ Choral Read   ❑ Lead Read

Word Study (Phonics)

Vowel Patterns 1 Lesson #: _____

❑ Card Sort   or   ❑ Spelling Sort

❑ Word Scramble   or   ❑ Word Ladders

❑ Writing (Sentence Dictation)

Comprehension (New Read)   Level

Before

❑ Previewing Vocabulary:_____

❑ Making Text Connections

❑ Making Predictions

❑ Previewing Text Structure (Nonfiction)

During

❑ Teacher Questioning

❑ Student Questioning

After

❑ Summarizing

❑ Using Graphic Organizers

to emulate. As you choral read with students, you have the opportunity to pull students through critical phrasing and expression. Additionally, these readers can benefit significantly from listening to and visually following along with you. Another technique involves reading a page and then asking students to read the same page to see if students can emulate you. Rereading can be conducted using these techniques, along with those mentioned previously, such as partner or whisper reading.

The following small group of transitional readers is well into this stage of development and is currently reading a Reading Recovery Level 15/16 book. This reading level is typical of an end-of-year first grader. In this lesson, rereading for the group includes several pages from the book that was read the previous day. These pages were selected because they contained a wide range of punctuation. Based on the teacher's observations, the students in the group are fluent with speed and accuracy, but they need practice with prosody. Therefore, the teacher has chosen to work on several pages with a wide range of punctuation rather than spending time rereading the entire book. Transitional readers often dislike rereading the entire text because they find it redundant. Another option is to select a poem to practice rereading that is at the appropriate instructional level. Poetry is an excellent way to improve phrasing in fluency. The poem could be used over several days as a rereading and lends itself nicely to choral reading or Readers Theatre where groups or individual students are assigned parts. As a general guideline, students should read a passage at least three times to increase their oral reading fluency.

Teacher: Yesterday we read the book *The Secret Cave*. I have chosen several pages for us to practice today that have a lot of excitement. Everyone turn to page 12. This is the part when Dad finally found Katie. I want you to follow along while I read the page first. Pay attention to how I change my voice when I come to quotation marks and other punctuation. If we don't pay attention to the punctuation, it makes the story or text hard to understand. It's important to read the story quickly and get the words right, but we must also pay close attention to the punctuation.

(Teacher models reading the page.)

Teacher: What did you notice about my voice when I read the page?

Mary: You changed your voice a little when you saw the quotation marks so it sounded different, sort of like the person was really talking.

Katie: And you also made your voice go up at the end when you read questions.

Teacher: Good. Now this time, we are going to read the page together so we can practice using expression. When you read, I want you to still be able to hear me, kind of like follow the leader.

(Teacher and students read chorally.)

Teacher: You did a good job. Now I want you to read it without me so I can hear how you sound.

(Students read chorally as teacher listens.)

Teacher: I can really tell that you are improving on using expression. Good job! I
             want you to reread this story with your partner when you have group today.

INDEPENDENT ACTIVITY ALERT

- Have students continue reading and rereading with a partner and independently. Each student or reading group should maintain an independent reading box. At this level, it is much easier to keep the box stocked with books previously read in group rather than new reads. If you choose to add new books that have not been read before in group, chose carefully and at independent levels well below the group's instructional reading level.
- Establish a poetry box of favorite poems read numerous times in whole group. Students can select a poem to reread or practice with a partner for a class performance.
- Have students record themselves reading on a regular basis. It allows students to listen to themselves and work on improving their oral reading fluency. (See CD 💿 for auxiliary materials including the Read and Reflect form to use in conjunction with recording.)

Word Study (Phonics)

Transitional readers are ready to study another important aspect of word recognition—the teaching of common, one-syllable vowel patterns. Success in mastering common vowel patterns depends on previous success in mastering consonant sounds, word families, and short vowels. For example, mastery of beginning consonants prepares students for short-vowel word family sorts. Success in reading and spelling the short vowels naturally leads into work on the five short-vowel patterns, and mastery of the short-vowel words brings essential knowledge to the common, one-syllable vowel pattern stage (Vowel Patterns 1). The sequence for word study in Vowel Patterns 1 is shown here:

a	i	o	u	e
cat	hid	mom	mud	red
make	ride	rope	cute	feet
car	girl	for	hurt	her
day		go	blue	he
		boat		
		look		
		cow		

Card Sort

The card sorting technique used with word families lends itself nicely to work with vowel patterns. The word study in vowel patterns begins by sorting each vowel pattern beginning with *A* pattern words in Level 1.

- Begin by placing the first three header cards on the table: *cat, make,* and *car.*
- Model the task by showing students that each of the words goes in one of the columns. Remind students that they must not only look at the words but also listen for the sound *a* makes in each word: *bad, same,* and *hard.*
- Students sort 4 words in each column with you modeling the correct response if necessary.

As a way to keep all students actively involved, the sorting activity can be turned into a game.

- Students take turns sorting one word at a time, then reading the column of words.
- If a student sorts the words and reads the column correctly, he or she receives 2 points (one for sorting and one for reading).
- If a student identifies another student sorting incorrectly, he or she receives 1 point.
- The player with the most points at the end of the game wins.

An advantage of this game is that all students are involved and paying attention; they love the competition. When students begin to recognize and verbalize the focus vowel patterns, replace the card sort with the Spelling Sort activity described next. Then, rotate between Spelling Sort, Word Scramble, or the Word Ladder activity. In addition, students should complete a dictated sentence daily.

Spelling Sort

This spelling sort activity follows the same guidelines as the spelling sort for word families and short vowels. In this activity, the students write the sorts on their Spelling Sort templates (see CD 🔘 for these word study materials) as the teacher calls out words that contain the focus patterns. As previously mentioned, there are two Spelling Sort templates: one for sorting three patterns and one for sorting four patterns. The four-pattern template is useful as students review and mix several vowel patterns. As a way to check and reinforce their work, the teacher sorts the cards on a tabletop sorting board as the students complete the spelling sort. At this stage, students write the focus patterns in the three or four boxes at the top of the template, depending on which one they are using. Figure 23 shows a completed spelling sort for three of the *A* patterns: short *a,* long *a*-consonant-*e,* and *ar.* Teachers should follow the word study scope and sequence provided for lesson pacing (see CD 🔘). Again, you may choose to skip lessons if the group masters the patterns before the suggested lesson sequence is complete, but do not remain in patterns longer than suggested. Transitional readers need to be exposed to all of the common vowel

FIGURE 23
Sample Spelling Sort

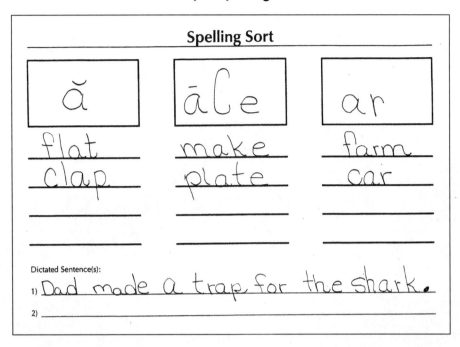

patterns as they navigate more complex text. Keep in mind that many of these readers will need to repeat the sequence for vowel patterns 1 more than once. Much of what students will read and write in the future will be words derived from these basic patterns, so teachers must be diligent, consistent, and patient as students work toward vowel pattern mastery. The "gift" of basic vowel pattern knowledge is crucial to continued reading and writing success.

Word Scramble

Word scramble at this stage is still a powerful activity to help students see relationships among patterns such as long *a*-consonant-*e*, long *i*-consonant-*e*, and long *o*-consonant-*e*. This activity enhances students' abilities to see relationships among words (see Figure 24). (See CD ◉ for word study materials including Word Scramble activities for each of the focus patterns.)

The following small group of transitional readers is completing a Word Scramble activity focusing on the *u* patterns that they are currently studying. Following the Word Scramble activity, the students will complete a dictated sentence that incorporates some of the focus patterns.

Teacher: We are going to do a Word Scramble activity today with the *u* patterns that we have been studying, so you are all going to need some letters to work with.

(Teacher distributes eight letters to each student.)

Letter cards: *u, n, e, r, t, g, h, b*

Teacher: Now you are going to make some words with *u* patterns. Listen carefully to my directions:

1. Make the word *rug.*

2. Change one letter to make *hug*.

3. Add one letter to make the word *huge*.

4. Change two letters to make the word *tune*.

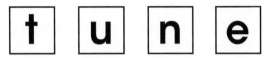

5. Drop one letter and change one letter to make *bun*.

6. Add one letter to spell *burn*.

7. Change one letter to spell *turn*.

8. Drop one letter to spell *run*.

(Students complete making each word as the teacher monitors and assists when necessary. Additionally, the Make and Write activity, which allows students to make and then write the word, can be used [see CD 🔘 for template].)

Word Ladders

Word Ladders can be used as an alternative to Word Scramble. Using the Word Scramble activities for Vowel Patterns 1, teachers call out the directions and students simply write the words on the Word Ladder template (see CD 🔘 for word study materials) by changing the letters. The words are written vertically to help students see the relationships among patterns in the words. See Figure 25 for an example of a Word Ladder for *u* patterns.

This activity serves as an excellent way for students to develop automaticity in recognizing these common vowel patterns in the context of reading and writing. Additionally, teachers can administer the spelling assessment for vowel patterns 1 to assess students' mastery of this basic phonics knowledge. Review the assessment results and plan for reteaching based on common mistakes. Keep in mind that for most students, it takes several times through the sequence before they master the patterns.

Writing (Sentence Dictation)

Sentence dictation for students at this level is quick and straightforward. The goal is to provide students with an opportunity to practice the focus word patterns in the context of writing complete sentences. To transfer students' word study skills into real reading and writing, it is critical for teachers to point out words in sentences that contain word patterns that have been introduced. In addition, call attention to word patterns in texts or other student-generated writing.

- Use the suggested sentences (see CD 💿 for word study materials including dictated sentences), or make up your own sentences that incorporate the focus vowel pattern words.

- Repeat the sentence several times, and then ask the students to repeat the sentence with you.

- As the students write the sentence (see Figure 26), assist any student who is having difficulty.

Teacher:	Our sentence today is *Sue rode the huge bus to her club*. Listen again: *Sue rode the huge bus to her club*. Now say the sentence with me, and touch each word on your fingers.
Teacher and students:	Sue rode the huge bus to her club.
Teacher:	Now pick up your pencils, and write the sentence. Think about all of the *u* vowel patterns as you write the sentence.
(Students begin writing.)	
Teacher:	(Reaches over to assist a child.) Lauren, do you remember the *u* pattern in the word *huge*?
Lauren:	Is it "long *u* sound"?
Teacher:	Yes, it is. Good for you. That is the sound for *u* but what is the vowel pattern?
Lauren:	Is it long vowel, consonant, e?
Teacher:	Very good.

FIGURE 25
Sample Word Ladder

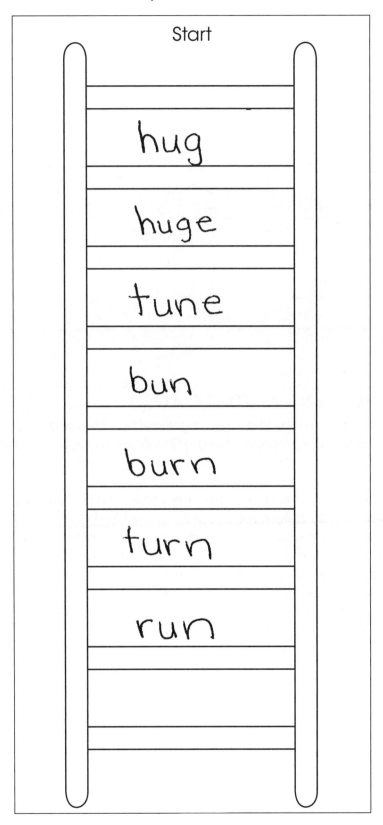

FIGURE 26
Sample Sentence Dictation

She rode a huge bus to her club.

INDEPENDENT ACTIVITY ALERT

- Allow students to play Memory using vowel pattern cards.
- Ask students to complete speed drills with a partner. Speed drills can be used to increase students' automaticity in recognizing word patterns. Often students can sort the patterns but have trouble writing them. This process requires visual memory of what the words and patterns look like so that students will be automatic in applying their knowledge in decoding new words. Students work in pairs and flash a stack of vowel pattern words to their partners. The students count the number of words read correctly in one minute and try to beat their best personal scores (Beat the Clock).
- Give each student a copy of the vowel pattern cards being studied. Have students sort the cards by pattern and stick them in a word study notebook.
- Have students choose two words from each pattern and write a complete sentence. Students can exchange their sentences with a partner to check for errors.
- Have students complete a Word Hunt to find words in previously read texts that have the same focus vowel patterns.

Comprehension (New Read)

The new read provides students with an opportunity to develop and apply decoding and comprehension skills. Specific strategies are used before, during, and after reading the text to support comprehension. Prior to on a picture walk, students make predictions about the story's content based on the title, the front cover, and the first few pages. The teacher also encourages students to make personal connections to the text. It's also important to preview the text structure prior to reading if nonfiction is being used. Prior to reading, preselected vocabulary from the story should be introduced and discussed.

There are a variety of oral reading alternatives to consider as students read the text selection, including choral reading, whisper reading, and lead reading or even partner reading. In addition, the teacher can take a turn reading so that students have a good model for improving their own fluency while focusing more on comprehension. Students who read aloud individually build fluency as well as gain valuable experience reading to an audience. When everyone is whisper reading at the same time, all the students are active readers with support given by the teacher. Reading with a partner offers students the opportunity to monitor the reading strategies used by another reader as they are put in a support role. Incorporating these reading alternatives helps students to remain focused as they interact with the text in a variety of ways.

During reading, the teacher asks students if they want to keep or modify their predictions and to explain why. At strategic points in the story (three or four times), the teacher stops to ask questions about what has happened so far (summarizing), what students think will happen (predicting), and what students remember (recalling). It is important that the new read be done with all students reading and contributing to the discussion to achieve maximum success with both reading and comprehension development. After reading, the teacher can use a variety of strategies outlined in this section to assist students with summarizing the story content.

Before Reading

Making Text Connections: In the following classroom vignette, students access their prior knowledge and make connections to a nonfiction book titled *Stormy Weather.*

Teacher: Today we are going to begin reading a book called *Stormy Weather.* I'm going to let you do a quick write for one minute and let you list all the different kinds of storms you can think of. Ready? Go.

(Teacher sets timer for one minute while students make a list of the kinds of storms that they know.)

Teacher: OK. Time's up. Let's start over here with Lucas. Tell us one kind of storm that you listed.

Lucas: I put a thunderstorm.

Teacher: (Starts a list on chart paper.) Good. Did anyone else put thunderstorm?

Harrison: Yes, I did too.

Teacher: All right. Harrison, did you have another kind of storm?

Harrison: What about a snowstorm?

Teacher:	That's a good one. Did anyone else think of that?
Karen:	No, but I put rainstorm.
Teacher:	OK, let's add that one to the list, too.

(Activity is completed with all students responding.)

Previewing Vocabulary: Prior to reading this nonfiction book, the teacher preselects and introduces vocabulary that is important to understanding the text's message. The teacher accesses background knowledge and helps students make connections.

| Teacher: | There are a couple of words in the text today that may be new to you. Here's the first one: *hurricane*. |

(Teacher writes each vocabulary word on a note card.)

Michael:	Oh, I've heard of those before but I didn't think about them being storms.
Teacher:	What do you already know about hurricanes?
Valerie:	Well, I know they have a lot of wind and can blow things down.
Teacher:	Good. When we read today, I'm sure that we will find out some more things about hurricanes.
Teacher:	Here's another word: *tornadoes*.
Lucas:	Oh, no. There's another storm we forgot, but I didn't think it was a storm. I thought storms had to have thunder and lightning.

Making Predictions: Predicting is only powerful as a comprehension strategy as the prediction is confirmed or modified during the read of the story. The teacher, therefore, includes only the predictions that students can confirm or change as they read the text.

Teacher:	Do you think that there has to be thunder and lightning to have a tornado?
Harrison:	I think it does. We usually have tornado warnings when there is a bad storm.
Teacher:	So you are predicting that there must be lightning and thunder. Does anyone disagree?
Michael:	I do. I saw these people chase tornadoes on TV and I didn't hear any thunder or see lightning.
Teacher:	Those are both good predictions based on what you already know about tornadoes. I think we will find out for sure when we read the book.
Helen:	I thought you also had to have thunder and lightning during a hurricane.
Teacher:	Good point. That's another prediction that we will check when we read the book. The last word we have is the word *dangerous*. Why do you think that this word will be used in the book?

Michael: Maybe because sometimes storms can be dangerous.

Teacher: I think you're right, Michael. I've seen pictures of storms on the news that looked very dangerous.

Previewing Text Structure: Before the group is ready to begin the book, the teacher walks them through the text structure. In narrative text, this would consist of a picture walk of the first few pages. For students, one of the hard parts about reading nonfiction text is how the book is set up. The teacher should review the structure including the table of contents, tables, graphs, picture captions, index, and glossary prior to reading. The reading strategies necessary for students to navigate nonfiction text hinge on their understanding of the text structure.

(Teacher gives out books.)

Teacher: What kind of storm is shown on the front cover of the book?

Harrison: It looks like a thunderstorm, but now I am thinking that it could also be a hurricane or tornado.

Teacher: Turn the page to the inside cover. Here we have the table of contents. How can this help us read the book?

Lucas: It tells us what kind of stuff is in the book.

Teacher: Yes, and it can help us think about the kinds of information that the author will share with us. What chapter would we look in to find out about the worst kinds of storms?

Valerie: I think it would be in the chapter about the biggest storms. It starts on page 10.

Teacher: There is something on the table of contents at the end that says "glossary." Does anyone know what a glossary is?

Michael: It's kind of like a little dictionary that just has hard words from the book in it.

Teacher: Yes, and it can help us if we run into a word and we aren't sure of what it means. Let's turn to the glossary on page 16. What words do we see here?

(The teacher and students review the words and then begin reading the text.)

During Reading

Teacher and Student Questioning: The teacher models questioning strategies and encourages students to question the text as an important part of comprehension. In addition, the teacher establishes a purpose for reading to help aid in students' comprehension of the text. It's also important that teachers vary the types of questions they ask. Students can answer literal questions directly from the text. Inferential questions require the information in the text *and* information that the students already know to come up with the answer. Application questions allow students to apply their knowledge to new situations or to make judgments.

———————

Teacher:	Let's all turn to pages 2 and 3. Take a look at the picture at the top of page 2. What's happening?
Harrison:	Well, it looks like a rainy day and maybe they are thinking about what they can do since they can't go outside.
Teacher:	All right. So, what do you think is happening in the picture at the bottom of the next page?
Helen:	It looks like they decided to play on the computer since they couldn't go outside.
Teacher:	Can you tell what is on the computer screen?
Lucas:	I think it's a picture of the world, but it's really hard to see.
Teacher:	Let's read these two pages together and find out why the children are using the computer.

(Teacher and students read chorally.)

Teacher:	Were we right?
Helen:	No, they weren't playing on the computer. They were looking on the computer to find out about the weather.
Teacher:	Turn to pages 4 and 5. What kind of storm do you see here?
Valerie:	It looks like a snowstorm. I've never seen a snowstorm like that. We don't ever get much snow here.
Teacher:	Well, the last time we had a big snow, you were still a baby and you don't remember it.
Teacher:	I want everybody to whisper read these two pages about snowstorms. If you come to a word you don't know, look at me and I will help you. As you read, find out what the difference is between a snowstorm and a blizzard.

(Students all whisper read while the teacher monitors them.)

Teacher:	The story tells us that snowstorms can be dangerous, but it doesn't tell us why. Use what you already know in your head and answer the question. Turn to your partner and share your answers.
Teacher:	Michael, what do you think?
Michael:	Well, for one thing you could freeze to death if your car broke down.
Teacher:	Yes, and that has happened to a lot of people when they got stuck on the road without warm clothes and food.

(The teacher guides the students through the text by using teacher questioning, by guiding student questioning, and by using a variety of oral reading techniques.)

After Reading

Summarizing: The primary comprehension strategy after reading is summarizing the information from the text. Summarizing can be accomplished with various activities including putting events in the proper sequence, completing story maps, comparing and contrasting, identifying main ideas and details, and so forth.

Teacher:	Let's go back to the vocabulary words we talked about before reading. The first word is *dangerous.* I want you to think of a sentence using the word *dangerous* that tells something about what we read in the book today.
Harrison:	We learned that some storms can be dangerous like snowstorms and hurricanes and tornadoes.
Teacher:	The next word is *hurricane.* Give me a sentence with the word *hurricane* that tells something we read about today.
Valerie:	We learned today that hurricanes start over the water before they come on land.
Teacher:	You really learned a lot today.

(The teacher finishes reviewing the other vocabulary words.)

Teacher:	As you leave group today, I want you to write a short summary about what you learned about storms today. Try to include at least three new things that you learned about storms that you didn't know before you read the book [see Figure 27].

See Figure 28 for a completed lesson plan for transitional readers.

FIGURE 27
Sample of Summarizing After Reading

FIGURE 28
Completed Reading Lesson Plan: Transitional Reader (Stage 4)

Group: _Pandas_   Date: _Nov. 4, 2008_

Fluency (Rereading) Level	Comments/Out-of-Group Activities
The Secret Cave (pp. 12 + 13) 16	Reread book with a partner.
☑ Whisper Read ☑ Choral Read ❏ Lead Read	

Word Study (Phonics)

Vowel Patterns 1 Lesson #: _22 u patterns_

❏ Card Sort or ❏ Spelling Sort

☑ Word Scramble or ❏ Word Ladders

❏ Writing (Sentence Dictation)

She rode the huge bus to her club.

Play Memory with a partner using U pattern cards.

Comprehension (New Read)   Level

Stormy Weather   16

Before

☑ Previewing Vocabulary: _hurricane, tornadoes, dangerous_

☑ Making Text Connections (Quick Write)

☑ Making Predictions

❏ Previewing Text Structure (Nonfiction)

During

☑ Teacher Questioning

☑ Student Questioning

After

☑ Summarizing

❏ Using Graphic Organizers

Students will write a summary about new information they learned about storms.

When to Move to the Next Stage

The move to the final stage, the Independent Reader stage, could best be described as a leap. To be prepared to move ahead, students need to automatically recognize numerous sight words and specialized vocabulary. These students also should be able to write dictated sentences containing varied vowel patterns with accuracy and confidence. Before progressing to the next stage, transitional readers must take the Stage 4: Vowel Patterns 1 assessment and pass with 80% accuracy or better. Independence—when students choose to read by themselves—is another indicator. Finally, the Reading Review should be completed to confirm that each student is reading at the appropriate instructional level, generally around late first grade or early second grade for average students.

Conclusion

Students' accomplishments in the Transitional Reader stage are extensive. The children have been transformed from being heavily dependent on the teacher to being confident readers. Developing strategies in decoding and comprehension have increased students' abilities to read independently. As these students transition to the Independent Reader stage, they will continue to focus on increasing their competencies in fluency, word study, and comprehension.

CHAPTER 8

Stage 5: Independent Reader

Characteristics of Independent Readers

Independent readers begin to exhibit characteristics of mature readers—reading with speed, accuracy, and proper expression. They read independently from a variety of genres and for a variety of purposes. In this stage, readers use diverse strategies as they cope with challenges in more difficult text. Independent readers can skim text quickly to retrieve information as well as infer (i.e., read between the lines and draw conclusions) in their efforts to comprehend text. Without conscious attention, these students perform multiple reading tasks—such as word recognition and comprehension—at the same time. Independent readers are equipped to negotiate a variety of genres, applying both decoding and comprehension strategies. Although they still need teacher-supported reading at their instructional level, they are capable of decoding and understanding text at the independent level.

Texts for Independent Readers

A variety of texts should be used with independent readers. Teachers should choose from a range of topics, formats, text types, and illustrative styles and use longer stories and chapter books with rich vocabulary and more fully developed plots. Teachers should avoid choosing too many long chapter books that will limit the selection in other genres. As educators, we sometimes feel that more accomplished readers simply need longer books. As reading maturity develops, readers will benefit from a wide variety of short pieces including a variety of fiction and nonfiction selections including editorials, poetry, and magazine articles. Most illustrations at this level are used to establish mood rather than to support the story line. Fortunately, many of the companies publishing leveled books have been attentive to the need for text variation in genres for independent readers, including many more nonfiction selections in their offerings. Teachers should always be mindful of the supports and challenges presented in each text selection. The following are appropriate leveled books for independent readers:

Leveling System	Book Levels
Reading Recovery	17–23+
DRA	18–38
Fountas and Pinnell	J–P

FIGURE 29
Reading Lesson Plan: Independent Reader (Stage 5)

Group:_____ Date:_____	
Fluency (Rereading) _____	Comments/Out-of-Group Activities
❑ Poem	
❑ Reread Text	
Word Study (Phonics and Word Features)	
Vowel Patterns 2 Lesson #_____	
Word Features Week #_____	
❑ Spelling Sort or ❑ Word Ladders	
or ❑ Word Scramble	
❑ Writing (Sentence Dictation) _____	
_____	
Comprehension (New Read) Level	
_____	
Before	
❑ Making Text Connections	
❑ Building Background Knowledge	
❑ Previewing Story Vocabulary _____	
_____	
❑ Previewing Text Structure (Nonfiction)	
❑ Making Predictions_____	
_____	
During	
❑ Teacher Questioning ❑ Student Questioning	
After	
❑ Summarizing (Main Ideas/Details, Compare/Contrast, Sequencing, Story Elements, Cause/Effect Relationships)	
❑ Summarizing With Vocabulary	

Instructional Strategies and Activities in the Independent Reader Lesson Plan

Fluency (Rereading)

At this stage, the lesson plan model has significant modifications to address the needs of these more accomplished readers as they move to a more intense focus on comprehending the text. Fluency remains important to independent readers, especially if students in the group have not met grade-level benchmarks for speed, accuracy, and prosody. In consideration of this, rereading may require more time in the lesson for less fluent readers. On the other hand, students who are meeting the benchmarks for oral reading fluency may not reread every day in group but will practice with a partner or independently out of group. Students could reread a part of a previously read text, but not the entire book. Another source for fluency practice is reading poetry. In my experience, students love the rhythm and rhyme and it is helpful as students work on phrasing and expression that is important in building fluency. In addition, I find that poetry provides vivid vocabulary and a wide variety of comprehension opportunities. You may choose to work on a piece of poetry for the week and therefore only 3–4 minutes of the lesson is devoted to fluency. As with text selections, vary the pieces to include humorous poems, seasonal poems, and even classical poetry. It is sometimes difficult to gauge the appropriate reading level with poetry, so teachers should always preview the poetry selection for appropriateness prior to introducing it to the students. If a particular piece provides too much challenge, simply replace the poem the next day with a less challenging piece. According to the National Reading Panel (NICHD, 2000), providing students with guided oral reading opportunities has a significant impact on word recognition, fluency, and comprehension through the eighth grade. Continuing fluency practice, therefore, should remain an important reading component whether practiced in group, with a partner, or independently. Regardless, fluent readers should be given ample time to read independently during the school day.

- Continue to incorporate teacher modeling in this part of the lesson to provide a fluent model.
- Use this opportunity to have students practice as though they were reading to an audience.
- Include poetry selections for fluency practice.
- Choose a page from a previously read text as a rereading piece.

The following small group is rereading a poetry selection as they practice their fluency. The teacher has chosen the poem "Never Take a Pig to Lunch" by Susan Alton Schmeltz and plans to use it all week as the fluency warm up that begins each lesson. The teacher knows that in the past this poem has caught the interest of even the most reluctant reader and it also contains a wide variety of punctuation for practice in prosody. The teacher introduced the poem in the previous lesson and provided a fluent model as she read the poem to the students. She also discussed some vocabulary words that she thought might be new to students. During this lesson, the teacher plans to read the poem with the students and have students keep the beat of the poem with their pencils. This activity will encourage phrasing in reading, which is important to the fluency process.

Teacher: Yesterday we read the poem "Never Take a Pig to Lunch." Today we are going to read the poem again and keep the beat of the poem with our pencils. I wrote another stanza to the poem about my dog. Let me show you how this works.

(Teacher begins by counting "1, 2, ready, go" and tapping the table lightly with a pencil. Then she begins reading a poem of her own and continues tapping her pencil along with the students to keep the beat of the poem.)

> Never teach your dog to read,
>
> Unless he is a special breed,
>
> One that schools permit inside,
>
> Where you can show him off with pride!

Teacher: Now let's try reading the entire poem together as we all keep the beat.

(On subsequent days, the teacher might include groups of students reading different verses of the poem in a Readers Theatre format.)

INDEPENDENT ACTIVITY ALERT

- Establish a poetry box of favorite poems read numerous times in whole group. Students can select a poem to read and record so they can assess their fluency.
- With one or more partners, students can practice and perform a reading using a Readers Theatre format.

Word Study (Phonics and Word Features)

Independent readers have successfully completed Vowel Patterns 1 and are now ready to proceed systematically through the study of less common vowel patterns. After completing the scope and sequence for Vowel Patterns 2, teachers can administer the spelling assessment to determine any needs for reteaching. Word study for independent readers concludes with common word features, which includes the study of common prefixes, suffixes, contractions, compound words, and homophones. See CD ◉ for word study cards, assessment, and word study scope and sequence.

a	i	o	u	e
r<u>ai</u>n	r<u>i</u>ght	t<u>o</u>ld		m<u>ea</u>t
b<u>a</u>ll	b<u>y</u>	m<u>oo</u>n		h<u>ea</u>d
s<u>a</u>w	f<u>i</u>nd	b<u>oi</u>l		n<u>ew</u>
		l<u>ow</u>		
		l<u>ou</u>d		
		b<u>oy</u>		

The activities that support the study of the less common vowel patterns include Spelling Sort, Word Scramble, Word Ladders, and sentence dictation. These activities were discussed in the previous chapters and will remain the same at this stage except the focus is now on Vowel Patterns 2. The first three activities should be rotated because there won't be time to complete all of them, but sentence dictation should be included daily. After students complete their study of Vowel Patterns 2 and move to the study of common word features, Spelling Sort and sentence dictation are the only two activities that are appropriate and therefore incorporated into each lesson plan. For this reason, this section focuses on providing an example of the Spelling Sort and Sentence Dictation.

The following small group of independent readers has successfully completed the Vowel Patterns 2 sequence and is currently working on suffixes in the study of common word features. The Spelling Sort is used as students sort and spell plural words based on the suffix needed: *s*, *es*, or *y* to *i* and add *es*.

Teacher: Today we are going to look at ways to make words plural. What does the word *plural* mean?

Melissa: Plural means that there is more than one.

Teacher: Yes, and depending on the ending of the word, there are different ways we make the words plural. Take a look at my sorting board. We will sort words by the different ways to make them plural. For some words, we only have to add an s to the base word to make it plural. For other words we have to add es or drop the y and change it to i before adding es. So, at the top of your Spelling Sort sheet, I want you to write s in the first box, es in the second box, and y/ies in the last box.

(Teacher observes as students fill in the boxes on the Spelling Sort template.)

Teacher: Now I am going to call out some words. You need to look at the three boxes and decide what you need to do to make the word plural. Would you have to add an s, es, or change the y to i and add es? The first word is *box*. What do you have to do to the word *box* to make it plural?

(Teacher observes as students sort and write the word under the appropriate box.)

Teacher: Chris, where did you write the word and why?

Chris: I wrote the word *boxes* under the es box because to make the word *box* plural you have to add es. I think that there is a rule that says if a word ends in x, you always have to add es to make it plural.

Teacher: I am so happy that you remembered that rule. Yes, the plural of *box* is *boxes*. We have to add es to *box* to make it plural.

Teacher: The next word I want you to write is *worry*. What do you have to do to the word *worry* to make it plural?

Katie: I put the word under s, but I'm not sure if you just add an s.

Teacher: What do the rest of you think?

Michael: I put *worries* under the last box because I think that if the word ends in y, you have to change the y to i and add es. I think that it is the same thing that you have to do for the word *baby*.

Teacher: Put your thumbs up if you agree with Michael.

(The other four students along with Katie give the thumbs up sign.)

Teacher: Sometimes it helps us to think of a more familiar word like *babies* to help us figure out how to make a word plural.

(Teacher continues the Spelling Sort until there are at least two words under each category. Figure 30 shows a sample spelling sort for plurals.)

Teacher: Now let's do a dictated sentence that includes some words that are in the plural form. The sentence for today is "The nurses took classes about taking care of babies."

(The sentence contains a plural that follows each of the three patterns. The teacher observes as students complete the dictated sentence. After the sentence is completed, the teacher points out the plural words and discusses the process used in making each singular word plural.)

INDEPENDENT ACTIVITY ALERT

- Have students complete Word Hunts for other words that include the focus patterns.
- Have students choose two words from each pattern and write their own sentences.
- Have students play Memory with a partner using the word study cards.
- Have students complete speed drills with the words from each pattern.

FIGURE 30
Sample Spelling Sort for Plurals

Spelling Sort

y to i	s	es
babies	nurses	foxes
worries	balls	dishes

Dictated Sentence(s):

1) The nurses watched all of the babies.

2) _____

Comprehension

Independent Readers are spending the majority of their small-group reading time engaged in comprehending new text. The lesson plan model provides explicit instructional recommendations as teachers guide students through before-, during-, and after-reading comprehension strategies. The following group of independent readers is beginning a nonfiction book called *Earthquakes and Tsunamis*. This book is grade level for late second to early third graders.

Before Reading

Making Text Connections/Building Background Knowledge: The first step in preparing students to read the text is encouraging them to make connections to the text with a personal experience. These connections might include a book that they have read on the subject or something they have observed or heard about. If students lack background knowledge about the subject, the teacher should share the information necessary for students to understand the text.

Teacher: Today we are going to begin reading about earthquakes and tsunamis. You have probably heard more about earthquakes than tsunamis.

Clint: I think there was a small earthquake in California last week.

Teacher: Several years ago there was a tsunami that killed a lot of people. I saved some pictures from a magazine that shows some of the damage.

(The teacher provides a way for students to connect to the text where background knowledge is lacking.)

Teacher: What do you already know about earthquakes and tsunamis? Do you know the difference between the two?

Debbie: I know that we have earthquakes in the United States but I don't think we have tsunamis. I think that you have to have an earthquake before you have a tsunami. Is that right?

(The teacher continues to lead the discussion to help students establish the connections that they can make to the text.)

Previewing Story Vocabulary: This nonfiction text contains a number of vocabulary words that will be important for students to know and understand. These words will also be important to the understanding of the text. When selecting key vocabulary words, consider the words that are important to the comprehension of the text.

Teacher: Let's look at some words that we are going to see in this book about earthquakes and tsunamis. The first word is *fault*. There are several meanings for this word like "It was your fault that we didn't get to go to the movie." We know this word *fault* has something to do with earthquakes or tsunamis. Does anyone know?

Andrew: Well, I think that a fault is like a crack in the earth.

Teacher: That's a good start. There are plates under the earth that move around very slowly all the time. Where the plates connect, there are faults. When the plates meet and one breaks, it causes an earthquake. Let me show you what that looks like.

(The teacher quickly sketches on a dry erase board to demonstrate. It is important that the students clearly understand the vocabulary words prior to reading the book. Avoid letting students getting into a guessing game with new vocabulary. If the students don't know the meaning of the words, simply tell them. Other vocabulary words that the teacher introduced prior to reading this book included collapse, jolt, plates, Richter Scale, earthquake, and tsunami.)

Previewing Text Structure: The hard parts about reading nonfiction text often include navigating the text structure. Before reading the text, the teacher should carefully preview the text structure so that students have an understanding of how to "read" the text (see Figure 31). These text structures might include the table of contents, graphs, picture captions, glossary, or index.

FIGURE 31
Teacher Working With Students in Group

Teacher: Let's take a look at the Table of Contents. It is important that we always take an in-depth look at this so that we can see how the book will unfold. By doing this, we will be better equipped to comprehend the text. We know from the title that the book will discuss earthquakes and tsunamis. I'm interested to see if the author will talk about them in separate chapters, or compare and contrast them in the same chapter. Look at the contents. What do you see?

Paul: The chapters look like the author first starts with chapters on earthquakes in the beginning of the book, and then the last part of the book is mostly about tsunamis.

Teacher: So we will need to remember that as we start reading the book. I also notice that the author has included a glossary and an index. Do you know the difference?

Rick: I know that the glossary is like a little dictionary with words from the book, but I'm not sure about the index.

Teacher: An index lists all of the important words or topics covered in the book. For example, if your teacher asked you to write a report about the San Andreas Fault, you could go to the index and see if it is an important topic in this book. It would tell you how many pages in the book are about this subject.

Making Predictions: Predicting prior to reading should be minimal, especially in nonfiction text. Predicting and confirming or changing predictions during reading is the most important part of using this strategy to increase comprehension.

Teacher: Based on what you know already know, what do you think the differences are between earthquakes and tsunamis?

Mary: All I know is that I think they happen in different parts of the world.

Teacher: As we read today, we will learn a lot more about the two.

During Reading

Teacher and Student Questioning: For this portion of the lesson, the teacher uses a variety of questioning strategies to encourage comprehension. As previously mentioned, these questioning strategies include literal, inference, and application questions. Additionally, the teacher encourages students to question the text as the book is read. Remember that questioning includes summarizing the text information at strategic points in the text. The teacher uses a Venn diagram during reading to identify important facts about earthquakes and tsunamis as well as examining comparing and contrasting the two topics.

Teacher: We know from the title of the book and the table of contents that we are going to be learning about earthquakes and tsunamis. So, as we read the text we are going to look for the important facts about earthquakes and tsunamis. We also want to examine how the two are similar as well as different. I'm going to draw a Venn diagram on the board that we will fill in as we read the text together. (See Figure 32 for sample Venn diagram.)

Teacher: Let's all turn to page 4 and read the introduction together. I will be the lead read and read out loud, and you whisper read along with me. As we read, let's look for ways that earthquakes and tsunamis are alike and different.

(Teacher and students read chorally. The teacher leads and provides a fluent model while engaging the students in the reading process as they all whisper read.)

Teacher: So, what causes a tsunami? Find the sentence in the text that answers that question.

(Students return to the text to identify the sentence.)

Teacher: Janet, will you read that sentence for us?

Janet: Yes, it is at the top of page 5. "When an earthquake happens under the ocean, it can make a tsunami."

FIGURE 32
Sample Venn Diagram

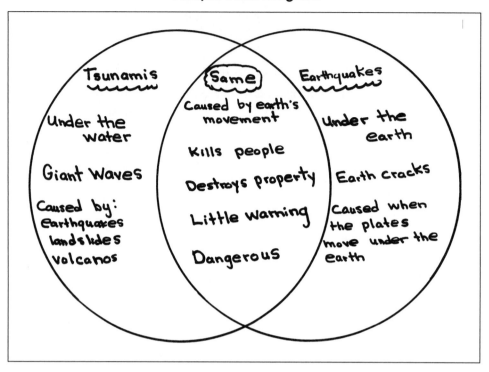

Teacher: When we can find the answer right there in the text it is called a literal question. We also see that there is a cause and effect relationship between the two.

Chris: The cause would be the earthquake under the ocean and the effect would be a tsunami.

Teacher: So what important details do we want to put on our graphic organizer about the two.

Leslie: For earthquakes, we should put that they shake and crack the earth.

Teacher: Good. Should I put that just in the circle for earthquakes or does it also apply to tsunamis?

Leslie: You should just put it down for earthquakes because tsunamis don't shake and crack the earth.

Susan: For tsunamis we should put that they are giant waves caused by earthquakes under the ocean.

Teacher: Are there any details that are important to both earthquakes and tsunamis?

Jennifer: Yes, they are both dangerous.

(This inferential question requires students to read between the lines to come up with the correct answer.)

Teacher: Can you think of other things that cause this much damage that people can be warned about before they happen?

(The teacher includes an application question that requires that students to apply their knowledge to another situation.)

Leslie: Yes, what about hurricanes? They can cause a lot of damage and the weathermen can warn people before they happen.

Teacher: Do you think that people get more warnings about earthquakes or hurricanes?

(The teacher continues questioning the students and encouraging them to ask their own questions as they complete the text.)

After Reading

Summarizing: Students can summarize the text using a variety of strategies. The teacher might choose to focus on identifying main ideas and details (especially in nonfiction text), comparing and contrasting, sequencing events, reviewing story elements, or focusing on cause and effect relationships in the text. This could be accomplished as the teacher leads an in-depth discussion with the students. Additionally, the teacher could choose to use a graphic organizer to give students a visual representation of the discussion. Another way to summarize is to revisit the story vocabulary and use it to summarize important text information. Independent readers are capable of responding in writing as a follow up to reading. The teacher can record these out of group assignments on the lesson plan. (See CD 💿 for reproducibles that support these comprehension activities.)

(The teacher has chosen to summarize the material with a graphic organizer. The Venn diagram gives important details about earthquakes and tsunamis and also gives a graphic representation comparing and contrasting the two natural disasters.)

Teacher: Today we finished reading our book on earthquakes and tsunamis. Let's take a look at our Venn diagram to review the important details that we have learned.

(Teacher leads discussion based on details on Venn diagram.)

INDENTED ACTIVITY ALERT

INDEPENDENT ACTIVITY ALERT

- Have students complete a writing assignment that connects to the text and supports comprehension. For example, ask students to write about the main character. Have them choose two character traits and give an example of each from the story.
- To aid in remembering vocabulary words, have students draw pictures of the words and then write sentences using the words (see Figure 33).

FIGURE 33
Sample of Independent Writing to Summarize

> # Natural Disasters
>
> Two Kinds of natural disasters are tsunamis and earthquakes. They are both dangerous and Kill people. The earth moves and causes big waves and Cracks in the earth. People should be careful. They should find a safe place.

See Figure 34 for a completed lesson plan for independent readers.

Conclusion

Although the Independent Reader stage is the last stage discussed in the Small-Group Differentiated Reading Model, this does not mean that independent readers are capable of reading any text presented to them. Fluency for a second-grade reader is very different from fluency for a fifth-grade reader. However, if we, as educators, are successful in bringing students to this basic independent level of literacy learning, the doors will open to a world of rich literary experiences.

FIGURE 34
Completed Reading Lesson Plan: Independent Reader (Stage 5)

Group:_____ Date:_____

Fluency (Rereading) _Never Take a Pig to Lunch_ ☑ Poem ❑ Reread Text	Comments/Out-of-Group Activities _Practice rereading poem with a partner._
Word Study (Phonics and Word Features) Vowel Patterns 2 Lesson #_____ Word Features Week # _4_____ ☑ Spelling Sort or ❑ Word Ladders or ❑ Word Scramble ☑ Writing (Sentence Dictation) _The nurses took classes about taking care of babies._	
Comprehension (New Read) Level _Earthquakes and Tsunamis_____ **Before** ❑ Making Text Connections ❑ Building Background Knowledge ❑ Previewing Story Vocabulary _fault, collapse, jolt, plates, Richter scale, earthquake, tsunami_ ❑ Previewing Text Structure (Nonfiction) ❑ Making Predictions_____ _____ **During** ❑ Teacher Questioning ❑ Student Questioning **After** ❑ Summarizing (Main Ideas/Details, Compare/Contrast, Sequencing, Story Elements, Cause/Effect Relationships) ❑ Summarizing With Vocabulary	_Summarize with vocabulary: Use each word in a sentence that tells something you learned from the text._

CHAPTER 9

Engaging and Managing the Rest of the Class During Small-Group Reading Instruction

The importance of small-group differentiated reading instruction cannot be emphasized too strongly. However, teachers have found it both difficult and time-consuming to manage the rest of the class in a meaningful way while they teach in small groups. In a balanced literacy model, independent practice is a critical component. This process allows students to practice and subsequently increase their literacy skills. So why do so many teachers feel that they are unsuccessful in planning for and implementing this independent practice? There are several factors that come into play.

For students to be successful in independent practice, they must be given tasks that allow for their success. In many instances, teachers assign all students the same tasks for independent practice. This occurs, in part, because teachers feel overwhelmed by the massive planning that they perceive in differentiating literacy activities for independent learning. Literacy tasks that are not geared toward each student's needs leave students unsuccessful and unmotivated, which in turn results in teachers spending too much time managing off-task behavior instead of teaching in small group. The goal for independent literacy activities is to ensure that *all* students are working at their level of learning and taking responsibility for their learning and behavior without extensive preparation by teachers. Planning for and engaging students in powerful research-based literacy activities can be accomplished more easily as teachers focus on simplifying the planning and monitoring process, intensifying the quality of the activities, and differentiating the materials students use to complete the activities. As each of these issues are addressed, teachers will be free to spend the time necessary to plan for and implement small-group instruction with the confidence that the rest of the class is engaged in quality literacy activities.

An enormous amount of material has been published in recent years that addresses models for engaging the "other students" during small-group instruction. The various names assigned to this independent practice are extensive: literacy centers, learning stations, literacy stations, literacy work stations, to name but a few. I believe, in some instances, that the planning and implementation required of these outside activities have consumed teachers' time and left them with little additional time for planning for effective whole-group and small-group instruction. Many experts encourage spending the first four to six weeks establishing the routines necessary to put these elaborate plans into action. Although I am a proponent of developing routines, this seems excessive. Are we perhaps forgetting that the most important part of teaching and learning will occur in whole- and small-group instruction led by the teacher? Should we really spend so much upfront time to teach routines? If it takes that long, are the routines and activities too complex? Although the first edition of *Small-Group Reading Instruction* delves into the topic of literacy centers, I also included activities that reinforced small-group instruction. My observations over the past five years have given me insight into the pros and cons of such models. Although the centers and stations are appealing, I began to ask myself the hard question: Is this the best use of the students' and teachers' time? With an ever-shrinking instructional day, I am convinced that we must reexamine the effectiveness of many of these practices and explore ways to simplify the process, intensify the quality of the activities, and differentiate the materials the students use to complete the activities.

Simplifying the Process

Let's start with the "simplifying" part of the process. I would like to begin by renaming the tasks that the other students practice independently as *literacy activities*. I prefer to call them *literacy activities* because the word *center* or *station* conjures up a visual for me that includes concrete places with color-coordinated, theme-based, teacher-made stuff. In other words, a room filled with cute activities for students that takes a huge effort on the part of teachers to create. Quite honestly, there are only a few areas of any classroom that need to be dedicated for a particular activity, such as a designated place for the classroom library or an area for listening to a recorded book. A literacy activity can take place anywhere, a designated area or any space including the students' desks.

Teachers can also simplify the process by taking a realistic look at the time frame for independent literacy activities. When students spend extended time each day in independent literacy activities, teachers may want to reexamine their daily schedules. Many teachers often overplan for the time students spend in independent practice and consequently extend the time so that students can complete the assigned tasks—however, think quality, not quantity. Another way to simplify the process is by reducing the number of completed activities or products that require grading. The process is as important as the product. Be selective in determining which products will be most useful and time efficient to monitor.

Intensifying the Quality of the Literacy Activities

What are the most effective activities for students to engage in independently? The answer is really quite simple: We look to the reading research–based components that should be practiced and reinforced: fluency, word study, vocabulary, and comprehension. The bottom line is that students need to be doing more reading, writing, and word study at their individual developmental levels. The next step, therefore, is to identify activities that provide independent practice of these critical components. As previously discussed, students become better readers by practicing and doing the work of reading. Although teachers often feel somewhat guilty in "only doing reading," when coupled with the appropriate book levels and both independent and partner reading the research base is being addressed.

Just as students perform at differing independent reading levels, we have also discussed developmental levels in word study. By following the word study scope and sequence described in this book and administering the spelling assessments, teachers will already be knowledgeable about individual student's word study levels. By applying the same philosophy for an independent word study level, it makes sense to simply practice the word study pattern that has been successfully completed in small group. For example, if the small group is working on vowel patterns 1 and are working on the *O* patterns, an independent word study level would be practice with the vowel patterns previously taught, which would be the *A* patterns and the *I* patterns. These patterns have been systematically taught in group, so then the focus can be shifted to independent activities that are engaging and gamelike to motivate students, as illustrated later in the chapter.

The independent writing can be trickier. What about the students who aren't yet writing? Drawing and scribbling are the precursors to writing, so for students who can't write they simply draw the responses. The writing that students complete should be centered on books that they have read or that you have read to them. Writing that encourages the comprehension of text is important. Gradually introduce and model written responses in whole group. Model this for students as you complete a shared writing activity in response to a read-aloud or shared reading. Personal journal writing could also be an option but not as the centerpiece for the writing-about-reading component.

Vocabulary for beginning readers first focuses on the first 100 sight words. Based on the knowledge level of the students, these words can be reinforced in independent practice. Listening vocabulary can be addressed through responding to read-alouds or stories heard on tape. Even nonreaders can draw pictures to depict words. Fledgling, transitional, and independent readers can use the story vocabulary from books read in small group as they summarize the story through writing.

Finally, comprehension for most emergent and beginning readers will be best practiced in responding to books they have heard. All students can respond with writing or drawing after a teacher read-aloud. Most emergent and beginning readers are still in the decoding phase of learning to reading; therefore, comprehension is not the central focus. Readers who have advanced to the subsequent reading stages will be able to write about the reading completed in the small group. As teachers plan with these research-based components in mind, students' learning will be intensified.

Differentiating the Literacy Materials

The word *differentiated* in and of itself is dizzying to many teachers. Differentiation brings visions of planning individual activities for every student and checking each and every activity daily to make sure that it was completed. Would it be possible to plan many of the same activities for students and differentiate the materials needed to complete them? For example, could everyone do buddy reading but use books at independent reading levels? In word study, could everyone complete a Word Hunt but hunt for words at their developmental level? I think that this can be accomplished and would lift a huge burden from the teachers, as well as motivate students with activities that they can complete successfully.

I recognize that this way of differentiating materials might not work in every case, but for the majority of them it would. In planning, therefore, include activities that could be differentiated by the materials used. The fewer activities that have to be planned for and taught, the more time teachers have to plan and deliver effective small-group instruction. Teachers can be more confident using activities that are differentiated and based on reading research. These activities should not be labor intensive for the teacher. If the students aren't doing most of the work in these independent activities, rethink the process.

In an attempt to differentiate the literacy activities completed independently, I have created weekly responsibility sheets based on students' developmental reading, writing, and word study levels (see CD ● for these sheets). These responsibility sheets provide the structure students need to complete independent tasks but also give students choices about the order in which they complete the activities. In *Teaching With the Brain in Mind*, Jensen (1998) writes about getting the brain's attention. He explains that to increase students' motivation and to keep their attention, teacher should provide choices and make learning more relevant, personal, and engaging. Choices don't necessarily mean choices in the activities themselves but can be as simple as giving students choices about what to do when. This arrangement also provides the added benefit of not being tied to a daily schedule. If the responsibility sheet is for the week instead of the day, it allows for absences, short days, and other unforeseen circumstances. When small-group reading time is over, you can proceed to the next lesson without waiting for those who are still working to finish up—consequently providing more time on instruction. Be sure to include some "what you can do when you finish" activities to your responsibility sheet options. This arrangement will be less stressful for both teachers and students.

Developmental Stages and Independent Literacy Activities

Independent literacy activities are dictated by students' developmental reading stages. Table 10 shows the developmental reading stages and their corresponding independent literacy focuses in fluency, word study, vocabulary, and comprehension.

Independent Literacy Activities for Emergent Readers

Providing appropriate literacy activities for nonreaders is challenging for most teachers. Emergent readers are limited to activities that do not require reading except in simple repetitive text. Teachers can use the activities listed on the weekly responsibility sheet as a guide (See CD ● for auxiliary materials including the responsibility sheets for readers of all stages.) A weekly responsibility sheet is preferable to a daily sheet because it gives students the flexibility to pick and choose the order in which the activities will be completed. Although many of these activities have been discussed earlier in the text, I feel that it is important for teachers to group and further discuss them in terms of planning for independent learning. For all auxiliary materials referenced throughout this section, please see CD ●.

TABLE 10
Focus of Independent Practice Based on Developmental Reading Stages

Reading Stage	Fluency	Word Study	Vocabulary	Comprehension
Emergent	Rereading Tracking print	Alphabet recognition and production	First 15 sight words	Listen to reading Drawing about reading
Beginning	Rereading	Beginning consonant sounds	First 50 sight words	Listen to reading Drawing and writing about reading
Fledgling	Rereading	Word families Short vowels	100 sight words	Listen to reading Writing about reading
Transitional	Rereading	Vowel Patterns 1	Visualize text vocabulary Summarize with vocabulary	Listen to reading Writing about reading
Independent	Rereading	Vowel Patterns 2 Common word features	Visualize text vocabulary Summarize with vocabulary	Listen to reading Writing about reading

Fluency

Fluency incorporates speed, accuracy, and expression. Emergent readers are in the beginning stages of fluency development and focus primarily on tracking print and concept of word. Independent reading group boxes should be established for each developmental reading stage that is represented in the classroom. The independent reading box should be filled with books previously read and reread in the group.

Buddy Reading: Each student should keep a Buddy Reading Log in a file folder in close proximity to the independent reading boxes. Using the Weekly Responsibility Sheet for Emergent Readers, the students check a box designated "Buddy Read" each time they complete a buddy read. The student fills in the name of the book, and the buddy who listened to them read signs the log. Figure 35 shows students engaged in buddy reading.

Read to Self: For this activity, students should self-select a book from the classroom library. Although the students may not be able to read the book independently, they may choose to "read the pictures." Books previously read aloud by the teacher are especially popular with students. Giving students some flexibility during the week about book choices can be motivating, especially to struggling readers.

Read With the Tape: The teacher records a repetitive book on tape so that the students can read along with it and finger point to the words. This is especially helpful to nonreaders.

FIGURE 35
Students Engaged in Buddy Reading

Word Study

Emergent readers recognize less than half of the alphabet; therefore, practicing the letters that have been previously taught in group is their focus. You may let students choose three of the four activities to give them some personal choice.

Memory: Each emergent reader is assigned a weekly partner for word study. Using the letters studied in the prior week, the students play Memory by making matches of upper- and lowercase letters.

Letter Hunt: In this activity, students search through magazines and newspapers for the focus upper- and lowercase letters. The students then glue the letters on a piece of paper as shown in Figure 36.

Read the Alphabet: Using a pocket chart and a set of upper- and lowercase letter cards, students line up the letters in random order on the chart (or on the floor if a pocket chart is not available). Include some punctuation marks to provide interest, as well as practice in adhering to punctuation in reading. Using a pointer, the students can "read" the alphabet stories that they create.

Letters Stamps: Using a set of alphabet stamps, students stamp matching upper- and lowercase letters.

Cut, Sort, and Stick: Give students a paper showing the upper- and lowercase letters that are currently being studied. Students cut the letters apart and glue the upper- and lowercase letters side by side.

FIGURE 36
Students Engaged in a Letter Hunt

Vocabulary

During independent practice, two forms of vocabulary can be reviewed: beginning sight word vocabulary and listening vocabulary.

Sentence Basket: Place the cut-up sentences students complete in small group in resealable plastic bags and place them in a sentence basket. Also, be sure to write the complete sentence on the outside of the bag. For this activity, the students choose one of the sentences in the sentence basket and put it back together. Then the students copy the sentence on a piece of paper and add an illustration. This activity allows emergent readers to focus on concept of word along with recognizing sight words.

Sight Word Memory: Using the focus sight words, students play Memory with a partner from their group. The word card pairs are then mixed up and turned over. Students then take turns flipping over pairs of cards to make matches.

Picture This: This visualizing activity can be completed with words from a teacher read-aloud or a book heard on tape. In this activity, the students simply draw pictures to represent the chosen vocabulary (see Figure 37). Keep in mind that the vocabulary words include listening vocabulary.

Comprehension

Although emergent readers are in the decoding stage of learning to read, they are also working on listening comprehension as they respond to read-alouds or books on tape.

FIGURE 37
Sample Picture This

Listen to Story: For this activity, students listen to a book on tape, usually in a listening area (which will be described later in the chapter). The listening area is valuable for a wide range of readers. You might want to schedule a particular day of the week that students are assigned to listen to the book on tape because space is limited in this area. If students aren't doing the reading themselves, the next best thing is for them to listen to a fluent reader. This increases motivation as well as listening comprehension and listening vocabulary.

Draw About Story: Students draw about the story they have heard. For example, students can complete a story map by drawing pictures of the main characters, setting, problem, and solution (see Figure 38). (See CD 💿 for a reproducible version of the story map, if desired.) Story maps support these nonreaders with graphic representations. Sequencing can also be a part of the activity; sequencing involves drawing the important events in the story in order.

Independent Literacy Activities for Beginning Readers

Many of the independent literacy activities for emergent readers are enhanced for beginning readers as they grow in their literacy knowledge. The focus for these independent activities continues to support the development of fluency, word study, vocabulary, and comprehension.

Fluency

Beginning readers need extended practice with reading simple text that contains repetitive sight words and words that are easily decodable. Rereading books at an independent

FIGURE 38
Sample Story Map

reading level provides students with the practice they need to develop as more fluent readers.

Buddy Read: Using books from the group's independent reading box, students re-read to a buddy of their choice. Students record their reading on the Buddy Reading Log, and the buddy who listens to the reading signs the log. The teacher may vary the number of buddy reads that is required weekly depending on the number of other required independent activities.

Read to Self: This activity allows students to choose books that appeal them. These books might include Big Books, content area books, or even newspapers and magazines. These materials will be too difficult for beginning readers to read, but this "picture reading" motivates students as they make personal selections.

Record and Reflect: Students record their reading of an independent-level book into a tape recorder. Then, students listen to themselves and use the Record and Reflect form to mark the appropriate smiley face as it relates to their self-evaluation. This activity should take place on a weekly basis.

Word Study

Beginning readers are in the process of completing their alphabet recognition and production along with sorting picture cards by beginning consonant sounds, including blends and digraphs.

Cut, Sort, and Stick: Using copies of the picture cards (see CD 💿 for these cards), students cut apart the picture cards that begin with the focus consonant sounds. The students then sort the picture cards by beginning sounds and glue them onto a piece of paper.

Picture Hunt: In this activity, students look through magazines to find pictures that begin with the focus beginning sounds. The students can also choose to draw pictures that begin with the focus consonant sounds.

Memory: Using the picture cards, students play Memory with a partner to make matches based on the initial consonant sounds.

Cut-Up Sentences: As a follow-up to the cut-up sentence activity completed in small group, the students cut up an individual sentence and glue it on a piece of paper. The teacher may choose to make the group sentence available as a means of self-checking. Then the students draw a picture that tells about the sentence (see Figure 39).

Vocabulary

For beginning readers, vocabulary focuses on automaticity in recognizing the first 50 sight words. In addition, these readers can enhance their listening vocabulary by drawing pictures to illustrate the words.

Sight Word Memory: Using the sight words mastered by the group, students play Memory with a partner from their group.

Picture This: Students draw pictures to show the meaning of words taken from the book on tape or the teacher read-aloud.

Flash Cards: Using copies of the sight word cards (see CD 🄯 for these cards), students flash the cards to a partner.

FIGURE 39
Sample Cut-Up Sentence

Comprehension

Beginning readers work on comprehension as they respond to stories. As they become more fluent, they respond to their own reading.

Listen to Story: Assign students to the listening area on a weekly basis to listen to a story on tape. This listening activity enhances listening vocabulary and comprehension.

Draw and Write About Reading: Beginning readers are also beginning to write. Some students still need to draw about their reading and gradually make the transition to more writing. Giving students a choice in the writing will be important to build confidence. Students should be held accountable for the skills that are developmentally appropriate in writing. Beginning writers should be able to represent beginning consonant sounds in words as well as writing some sight words. Thus, beginning readers can draw and write about the setting, characters, problem, or solution of a story.

Independent Literacy Activities for Fledgling, Transitional, and Independent Readers

Students in the Fledgling, Transitional, and Independent reading stages are able to complete most of the same activities, although the materials in fluency, word study, and comprehension should be differentiated to meet the needs of each group.

Fluency

Rereading leveled text allows these readers to develop their oral reading fluency, speed, accuracy, and expression, which are important as these readers navigate more complex text.

Buddy Read: Students continue to use the Buddy Reading Log to practice their oral reading fluency. The books used for this activity are taken from each group's independent reading box, which is made up of books previously read in group.

Record and Reflect: Students read an independent-level book into a tape recorder. Then, students listen to themselves and use the Record and Reflect form to mark the appropriate smiley face as it relates to their self-evaluation.

Read to Self: As students become more confident readers, self-selected reading becomes more prevalent, as shown in Figure 40. Students are now able to select books that have not been previously read in group, so teachers should provide a classroom leveled library where students can self-select new reads at an appropriate independent level.

Word Study

These readers are progressing through a systematic study of patterns in words. Although these readers will be at different points in their word study sequence, the following independent activities work well in each stage of reading development. By providing students with their own copies of the word study cards, they will have numerous opportunities for independent activities. All word study cards can be found on the CD 💿.

Memory: Use the word study cards for this activity, including word families, short vowels, vowel patterns, and common word features. With a partner, students make matches with words that include a common word pattern.

FIGURE 40
Students Self-Selecting Their Reading

Sentences: Students choose two words from each of the focus patterns and write a sentence with each word.

Word Hunt: Students can do Word Hunts using newspapers, text, and magazines to look for additional words that contain the focus patterns.

Cut, Sort, and Write: Using copies of the word study cards, students cut apart the cards, sort them by common pattern, and write the sorts.

Beat the Clock: In this activity, pairs of students work together as they quickly flash the word study cards to their partners. The students set a timer for one minute and record the number of words they read correctly in this time frame. Students can record their scores on the template found on the CD 💿.

Alternative Activities With Word Study Cards: Using the word study cards, students can make plurals of as many words as possible. Also, students can add prefixes or suffixes to as many words as possible.

Vocabulary

For these readers, vocabulary is studied from the text and from word study patterns. In addition, fledgling readers solidify automaticity of the first 100 sight words.

Summarize With Vocabulary: Using the focus text vocabulary for the group, students write a sentence using each vocabulary word that tells something about the text.

Picture This: In a word study journal, students record new words and provide drawings and a sentence for each word.

Comprehension

For these readers, comprehension is enhanced as they respond in writing to books they are currently reading in group, a book on tape, or a teacher read-aloud.

Listen to Reading: Assign students a weekly time to listen to a story on tape. This book can be above the reading level of most students in the class and is instrumental in increasing listening comprehension and vocabulary.

Write About Reading: Students summarize the information from the reading. See CD ⊙ for auxiliary instructional materials that support summarizing in both fiction and nonfiction. There are forms to support sequencing events, finding main ideas and details, comparing and contrasting, finding cause-and-effect relationships, and summarizing the story structure.

Classroom Organization That Supports Independent Practice

Classroom organization is critical to the success of the independent activities. The classroom arrangement should be simple and uncluttered, and materials should be easily accessible to students. The following areas can help maintain this organization.

Independent Reading Area

Independent reading areas include spaces in the classroom that are designated for storing materials used for independent literacy practice. A word of caution: Keep it simple. These areas can house classroom reading libraries and include content area books, leveled books, independent group reading boxes, magazines, newspapers, favorite storybooks, and even poetry. Including comfortable seating in this area encourages extended reading opportunities for students. In addition, the reading area also should house a box of file folders for the Buddy Reading Logs so that students can access them easily.

The teacher may also consider using this as an area to house summarizing activities as students write about reading. Instead of making individual copies of the activities for students to complete, simply put the activities in sheet protectors and let the students use them as models. This also allows students choices in how they respond in writing. Model each of the activities in whole group so that the students are familiar with all of the activities. Try adding one new writing activity per week after you have modeled it with a read-aloud.

Word Study Area

It also is helpful to establish an area for word study activities. This area can house sentence baskets, timers, sets of high-frequency words, alphabet letters or letter cards, and sets of word study cards that are used for games. A pocket chart also can be included for creating alphabet stories and sorting word study cards. Boxes filled with old magazines and newspapers also are helpful as students complete picture and Word Hunts. Each student also should keep a word study journal to record sorts, sentences, vocabulary, and writing about reading in the word study area.

This area also can include a file box so that students can store their independent responsibility sheets that they use to track independent activities. This will also give the teacher easy access to the folders to monitor individual student progress.

Listening Area

The listening area can accommodate the materials necessary to listen to a story on either a CD or tape. I find it easier to simply keep the volume turned down rather than worry about headphones that are constantly not working or tangled up. If you are assigning a follow-up activity in vocabulary or comprehension in response to listening, you will need a place to display or store the activity.

Record and Reflect Area

This area can simply consist of an individual student desk with a tape recorder. Keep a file folder for each student so that they can store their Record and Reflect forms here.

Establishing Routines

The success of independent literacy activities depends, to a great extent, on how well the teacher establishes routines with the students. From the first day of school, begin getting your students acclimated to working independently. Start by spending short periods of time with the small group and perhaps do only one or two parts of the reading lesson. Make sure that everyone understands this essential rule: Never disturb the teacher during small-group reading instruction unless someone is sick or injured. Try placing a strip of tape on the rug close to your group and tell students to stand on the tape if there is an emergency. If you see that the students are not sick or injured, let them stand there and, after a while, they will return to their activities. Other suggestions to prevent interruptions include the following:

- Practice some "what if" scenarios with students at the beginning of the year. For example, what if you forget how to turn on the tape recorder? What should you do? As situations arise in the beginning of the year, take the time to teach students how to respond to the issue and hold them accountable the next time it happens.

- Keep a small lamp on your table. If the light is on, students should not disturb the teacher. This serves as a constant visual reminder, too.

- Discuss with students the importance of their special "small-group time" and how you want everyone to respect the time others are spending with the teacher.

- Put on a funny hat when you are in reading group. This will act as a signal that you are not to be disturbed.
- Be clear about instructions and expectations. If you are requiring a finished product as an outcome of an activity, give students models or rubrics that establish models.

The upfront time spent in practicing these routines will pay big dividends. One of the best ways to differentiate independent literacy activities is to teach the same routines and activities and then differentiate the materials based on the developmental reading stages of the students.

Conclusion

Each piece of the balanced literacy model serves an important purpose, including whole-group, small-group, and independent practice as well as reading intervention as needed. Perhaps the most challenging piece of the puzzle for teachers is in providing appropriate independent literacy learning opportunities. Students need to be engaged in independent activities that continue to support their growth in fluency, word study, vocabulary, and comprehension.

The model outlined for independent literacy activities is more than just a management system—it is a research-based literacy framework for independent practice. As teachers simplify the planning process, instruction will become more focused and easier to manage. The success of independent student learning will lie in the explicit modeling and practice of each activity and the differentiation of materials that support students in varied levels of literacy development. This will provide the framework of meaningful literacy activities tailored to meet the developmental reading levels of all students.

The purpose for independent practice is to free the teacher to provide differentiated instruction in small groups. With an ever-shrinking instructional day, it no longer makes sense to "drop everything and read." Independent practice should take place while the teacher is engaged in small-group instruction. As we examine the important literacy pieces that should be included in independent practice, we must still look to reading research–based practices. It is therefore important that students engage in literacy activities that support oral reading fluency, word study including phonics and phonemic awareness, vocabulary, and comprehension. Keeping the activities simple yet powerful and achievable for the individual students will give teachers the opportunity to spend more time on planning and implementing small-group differentiated reading instruction. The orchestration of all of the important reading research–based components in regards to whole-group, small-group, and independent practice will be the key to growing literacy skills.

Building a Framework for Early Reading Success

Few would argue that the educational future for many students is grounded in early reading success. Recently, there has been an unprecedented focus on the teaching of beginning reading, but most would agree that we are still failing far too many students. Without solid, research-based instruction delivered in a systematic format, we will continue to miss the mark for many struggling readers. Textbook companies have been quick to respond to federal mandates for research-based materials with boxed reading programs. Unfortunately, boxed reading programs will never be the answer to addressing the needs of a wide range of readers in the classroom. Although basal readers are successful in providing the framework for whole-group instruction, the materials necessary and knowledge of the developmental reading process cannot be overlooked in providing effective, differentiated reading instruction.

The teaching of reading is a complex process at best. To become an effective teacher of reading, a teacher must first be cognizant of the reading research–based components of effective reading instruction. Additionally, the teacher must be skillful in planning for both whole-group and small-group differentiated reading instruction. In whole-group instruction, the venues for teaching reading to a wide range of readers are embedded in reading aloud and shared reading. This allows the teacher to address grade-level standards and to share text that is above the reading level of many students. On the other hand, small-group differentiated reading instruction provides the venue for addressing the instructional reading and word study levels of all students. With an ever-shrinking instructional day, teachers must carefully examine every reading activity in terms of the research and the developmental needs of all readers. The developmental lesson plans in this book will assist teachers in this process.

Every child deserves the opportunity to receive quality reading instruction—reading instruction that transforms him or her into a competent reader. Reading is the key that unlocks future educational opportunities for all students. Although all students may not elect to attend a college or university, most will join the workforce and become parents of children who will need to be read to and nurtured in a literate environment.

Although some children learn to read prior to explicit reading instruction, many do not. For these children, there is not a classroom moment to waste. If we are to accomplish the lofty goal of making every child a successful reader, educators must be diligent in designing and implementing comprehensive reading programs. Small-group differentiated reading instruction can be used to effectively address the potential problems and serve the important purpose of reducing reading failure. Grouping students of similar reading abilities helps teachers plan instruction that best matches students' needs. This reading instruction must be consistent and provide students with opportunities to engage in contextual reading as well as systematic word study that is carefully paced to maximize learning opportunities. When children have a strong literacy foundation, the educational opportunities become endless.

This book presents step-by-step lesson plans reflecting the developmental stages of the reading process that will assist teachers in planning for meaningful instruction in primary-grade classrooms. Although this book contains many familiar, research-based strategies, it is not in these individual strategies alone that we find the strength of the Small-Group Differentiated Reading Model. The power is found in the way in which these strategies are pieced together and structured to support one another.

I believe that teachers are in need of useful, research-based models that can be easily adapted for classroom implementation. My observations have led me to believe that most teachers are overwhelmed by the demands of students, parents, administrators, and even legislators, leaving little time for reading and studying the current research. Expecting teachers to develop quality, research-based instructional models prior to actually teaching is like asking actors to perform Shakespeare but to write the play first.

There is no reading manual that can accurately tell a teacher everything to say or do. In my attempt to simplify the very complex reading process, I acknowledge and emphasize the unique needs of each student. I do, however, feel that the approach presented in this book might help lay the foundation on which teachers can begin to build effective reading programs for all students. We can no longer be content in only addressing the needs of struggling readers. Federal mandates require that all students show growth in the area of reading. This will require that teachers recognize the need for providing differentiated instruction to students performing above, on, and below grade level. It is, therefore, even more urgent that teachers recognize the stages of reading development and deliver instruction that allows all readers to grow. I am first and foremost a teacher. Like most teachers, I am seeking solutions to teach all children how to read. Given appropriate instruction, I am confident that we can significantly increase the number of students reading at or above grade level by the end of third grade. My hope is that teachers will embrace the material in this book that will empower them to be successful teachers of reading for all students.

REFERENCES

Armbruster, B.B., Lehr, F., & Osborn, J.M. (2001). *Put reading first. The research-building block for teaching children to read.* Jessup, MD: National Institute for Literacy.

Bear, D.R., Invernizzi, M., & Johnston, F. (2004). *Words their way: Word study for phonics, vocabulary and spelling instruction* (3rd ed.). Upper Saddle River, NJ: Prentice Hall.

Blachowicz, C.L.Z., & Fisher, P. (2000). Vocabulary instruction. In M.L. Kamil, P.B. Mosenthal, P.D. Pearson, & R. Barr (Eds.), *Handbook of reading research* (Vol. 3, pp. 503–523). Mahwah, NJ: Erlbaum.

Block, C.C., & Pressley, M. (2000). *Comprehension instruction: Research-based practices.* New York: Guilford.

Chall, J.S. (1987). The importance of instruction in reading methods for all teachers. In R.F. Bowler (Ed.), *Intimacy with language: A forgotten basic in teacher education* (pp. 15–23). Baltimore: Orton Dyslexic Society.

Chard, D.J., Vaughn, S., & Tyler, B.J. (2002). A synthesis of research on effective interventions for building reading fluency with elementary students with learning disabilities. *Journal of Learning Disabilities, 35*(5), 386–406.

Clay, M.M. (1979). *Reading: The patterning of complex behaviour.* Auckland, New Zealand: Heinemann.

Clay, M.M. (1993). *Reading Recovery: A guidebook for teachers in training.* Portsmouth, NH: Heinemann.

Dowhower, S.L. (1987). Effects of repeated reading on second-grade transitional readers' fluency and comprehension. *Reading Research Quarterly, 22*(4), 389–406. doi:10.2307/747699

Farstrup, A.E., & Samuels, S.J. (2002). *What research has to say about reading instruction* (3rd ed.). Newark, DE: International Reading Association.

Fountas, I.C., & Pinnell, G.S. (1996). *Guided reading: Good first teaching for all children.* Portsmouth, NH: Heinemann.

Fountas, I.C., & Pinnell, G.S. (2003). *Phonics lessons: Letters, words, and how they work, grade 2.* Portsmouth, NH: Heinemann.

Gill, J.T. (1992). The relationship between word recognition and spelling. In S. Templeton & D. Bear (Eds.), *Development of orthographic knowledge and the foundations of literacy* (pp. 79–104). Hillsdale, NJ: Erlbaum.

Goswami, U. (2002). Early phonological development and the acquisition of literacy. In S.B. Neuman & D.K. Dickinson (Eds.), *Handbook of early literacy research* (pp. 111–125). New York: Guilford.

Harvey, S., & Goudvis, A. (2002). *Comprehension strategies that work.* York, ME: Stenhouse.

Hasbrouck, J., & Tindal, G.A. (2006). Oral reading fluency norms: A valuable assessment tool for reading teachers. *The Reading Teacher, 59*(7), 636–644. doi:10.1598/RT.59.7.3

Henderson, E. (1990). *Teaching spelling* (2nd ed.). Boston: Houghton Mifflin.

Hennings, D.G. (2000). Contextually relevant word study: Adolescent vocabulary development across the curriculum. *Journal of Adolescent & Adult Literacy, 44*(3), 268–279.

Jensen, E. (1998). *Teaching with the brain in mind.* Alexandria, VA: Association for Supervision and Curriculum Development.

Kuhn, M.R., & Stahl, S.A. (2003). Fluency: A review of developmental and remedial processes. *Journal of Educational Psychology, 95*(1), 3–21. doi:10.1037/0022-0663.95.1.3

Learning First Alliance. (1998). *Every child reading: An action plan.* Washington, DC: Author.

Lombardino, L., Defillipo, F., Sarisky, C., & Montgomery, A. (1992, June). *Kindergarten children's performance on the Early Reading Screening Instrument.* Paper presented at the annual convention of the American Speech-Language-Hearing Association, San Antonio, TX.

Morris, D. (1993). *A selective history of the Howard Street Tutoring Program (1979–1989)* (Report

No. SC011220). Chicago: Chicago Public Schools. (ERIC Document Reproduction Service No. ED355473)

Morris, D. (1998). Assessing printed word knowledge in beginning readers: The Early Reading Screening Instrument (ERSI). *Illinois Reading Council Journal, 26*(2), 30–39.

Morris, D. (1999). *The Howard Street tutoring manual: Teaching at-risk readers in the primary grades*. New York: Guilford.

Morris, D., & Perney, J. (1984). Developmental spelling as a predictor of first-grade reading achievement. *The Elementary School Journal, 84*(4), 440–457. doi:10.1086/461375

Morris, D., Tyner, B., & Perney, J. (2000). Early Steps: Replicating the effects of a first-grade reading intervention program. *Journal of Educational Psychology, 92*(4), 681–693. doi:10.1037/0022-0663.92.4.681

National Center for Education Statistics. (2001). *The nation's report card: Fourth-grade reading highlights 2000* (NCES 2001-513). Washington, DC: U.S. Department of Education.

National Institute of Child Health and Human Development. (2000). *Report of the National Reading Panel. Teaching children to read: An evidence-based assessment of the scientific research literature on reading and its implications for reading instruction* (NIH Publication No. 00–4769). Washington, DC: U.S. Government Printing Office.

Neuman, S.B., & Dickinson, D.K. (Eds.). (2002). *Handbook of early literacy research*. New York: Guilford.

Perney, J., Morris, D., & Carter, S. (1997). Factorial and predictive validity of first graders' scores on the Early Reading Screening Instrument. *Psychological Reports, 81*(1), 207–210.

Reitsma, P. (1988). Reading practice for beginners: Effects of guided reading, reading-while-listening, and independent reading with computer-based speech feedback. *Reading Research Quarterly, 23*(2), 219–235. doi:10.2307/747803

Santa, C.M. (1999). *Early Steps: Learning from a reader*. Kalispell, MT: Scott.

Santa, C.M., & Høien, T. (1999). An assessment of Early Steps: A program for early intervention of reading problems. *Reading Research Quarterly, 34*(1), 54–79. doi:10.1598/RRQ.34.1.4

Texas Reading Initiative. (n.d.). *Differentiated instruction*. Retrieved October 27, 2002, from www.tea.state.tx.us/reading/model/diffinst.html

Tierney, R.J., & Shanahan, T. (1991). Research on the reading–writing relationship: Interactions, transactions, and outcomes. In R. Barr, M.L. Kamil, P.B. Mosenthal, & P.D. Pearson (Eds.), *Handbook of reading research* (Vol. 2, pp. 246–280). White Plains, NY: Longman.

Vygotsky, L.S. (1978). *Mind in society: The development of higher psychological processes* (M. Cole, V. John-Steiner, S. Scribner, & E. Souberman, Eds. & Trans.). Cambridge, MA: Harvard University Press.

INDEX

Note. Page numbers followed by *f* or *t* indicate figures or tables, respectively.